AF291417

Matthew Chen

The Weekender

# SINGAPORE

**COLLECTIVE SHORTS**
*by* NHP PUBLISHING

Looking out of the window as the airplane descends towards Singapore, one will be greeted by the sight of shipping vessels lining the Straits. After all, Singapore has always been an important trading port since pre-colonial days. For decades now, Singapore has been a melting pot of cultures, where the West meets the East. This integration of Western and Eastern influences has since developed the rich cultural and social fabric that we see today. Despite living abroad for a couple of years, Singapore will always be home to me, and is where my roots lie.

As a young nation, short of sixty years of independence, Singapore has grown to be one of the world's most affluent and vibrant cities. Whilst it's true that Singapore is a fast-paced and built-up country, the city-state has much more to offer than its already known attractions. There is juxtaposition in the landscape, and amalgamated boundaries between the contemporary and historic, man-made and nature.

Lesser known to the world, Singapore was designed as a garden city with pockets of green spaces which offer relief from the hardscape. In recent years, citizens have placed emphasis on a holistic approach to lifestyle, adopting a slower-paced lifestyle focusing on personal wellness.

As a photographer, I offer a more laidback and tangential perspective of Singapore. This book is conceptualized with the idea of spending a long weekend in Singapore, and has been divided into four chapters: Thursday, Friday, Saturday and Sunday. It features some of my most favourite and frequented spots in town, with a variety of both local and tourist sights, and a medley of different cuisines which I hope, throughout the subsequent pages, will attract you to visit my city state soon.


Matthew Chen

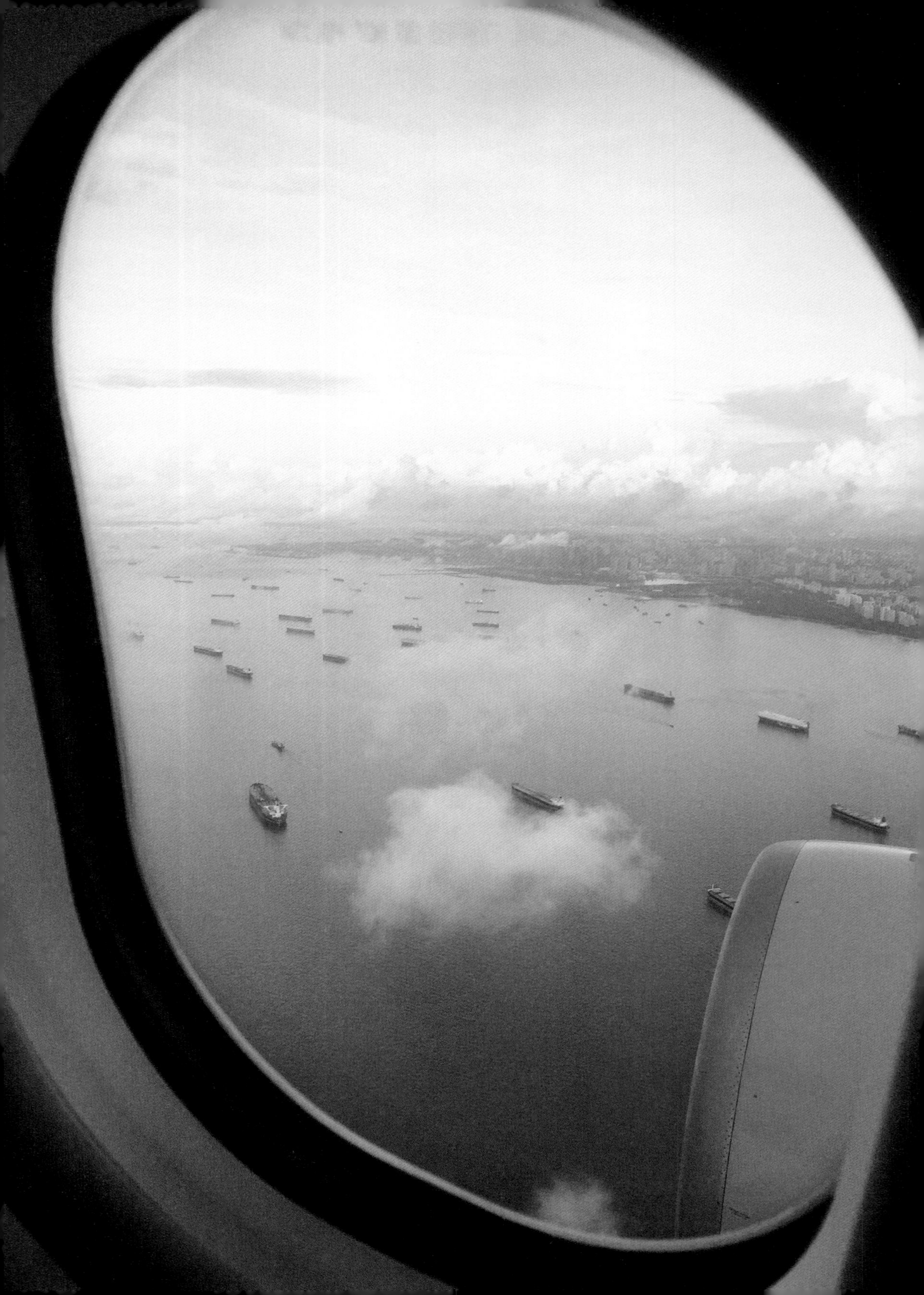

Thursday

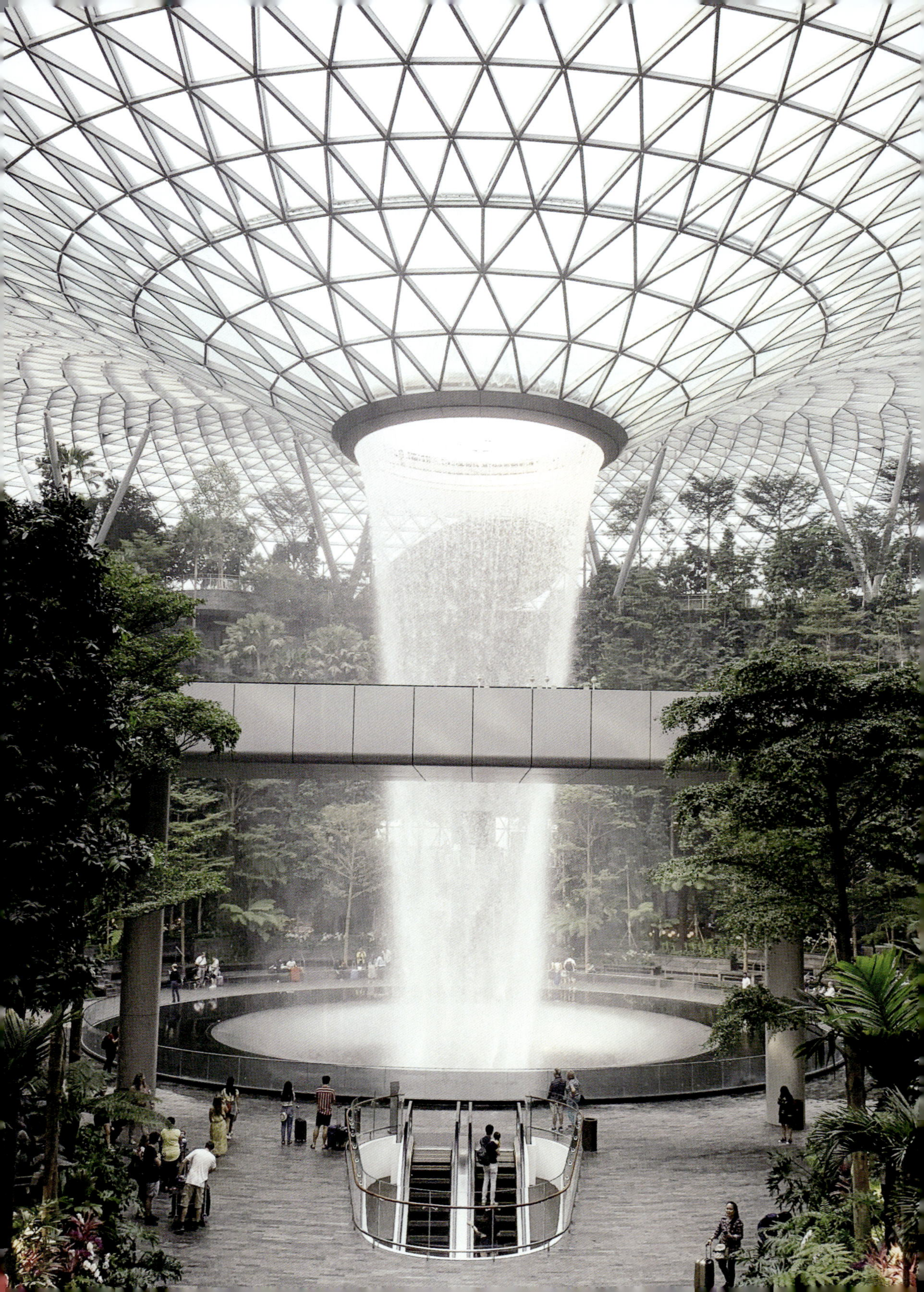

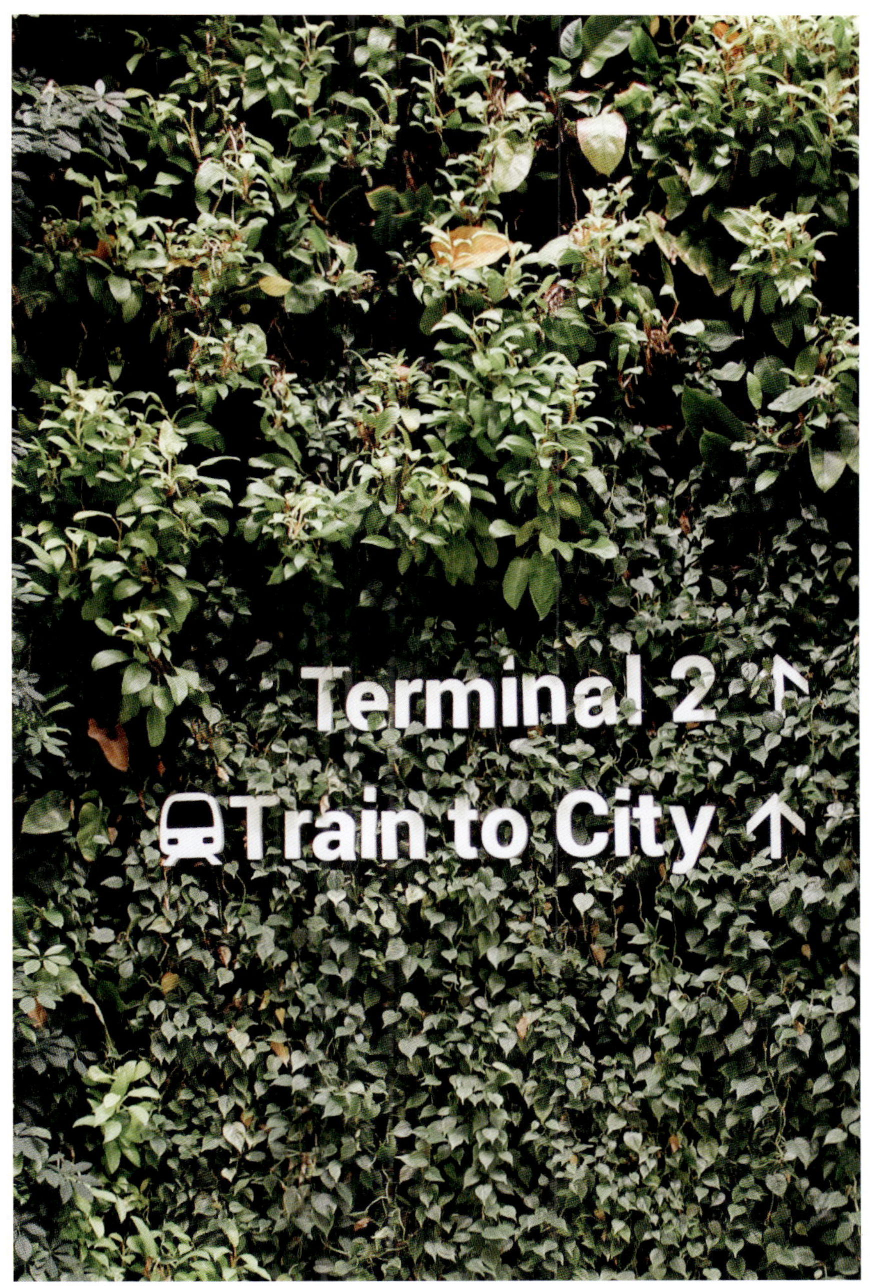

Terminal 2
Train to City

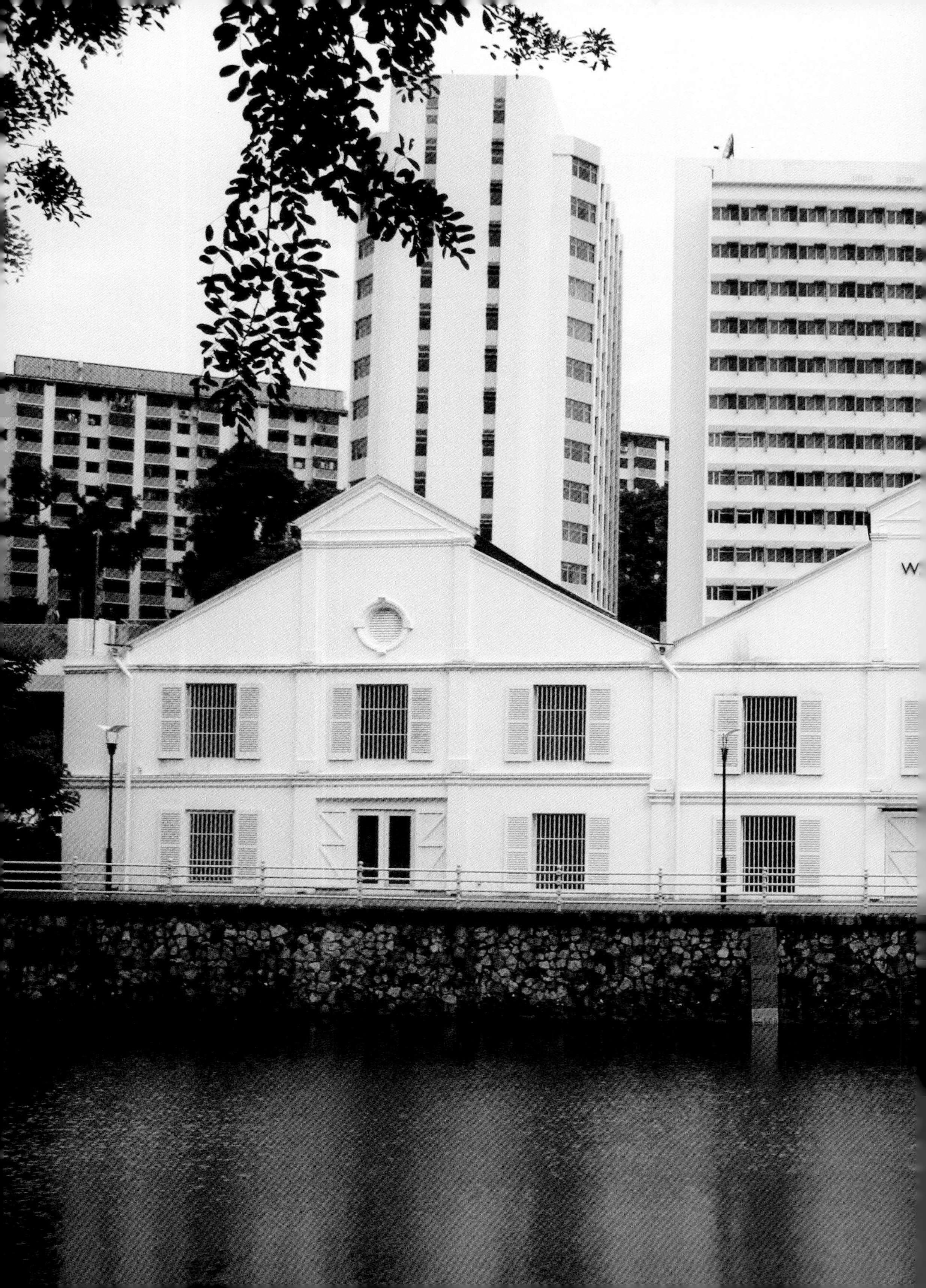

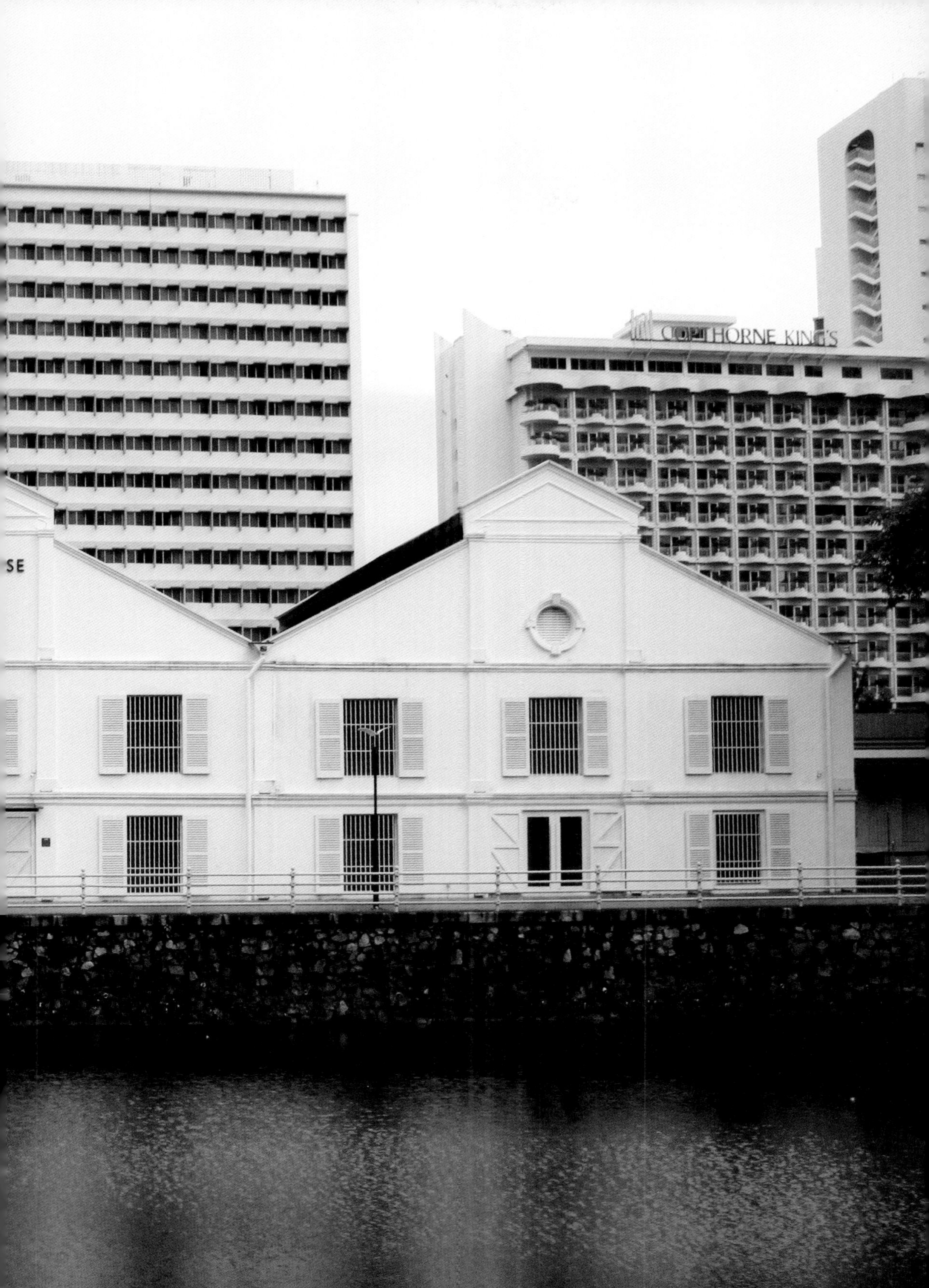

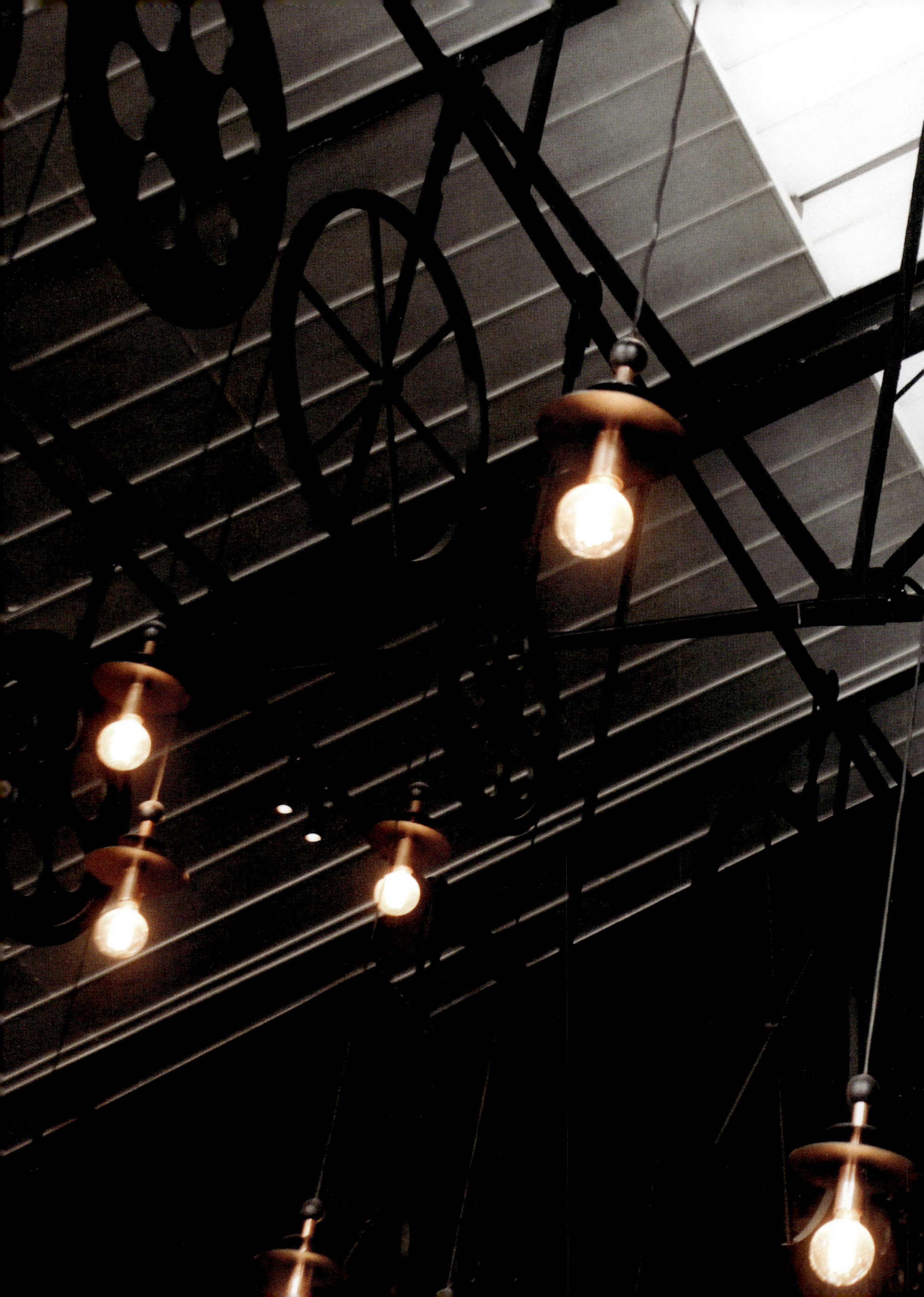

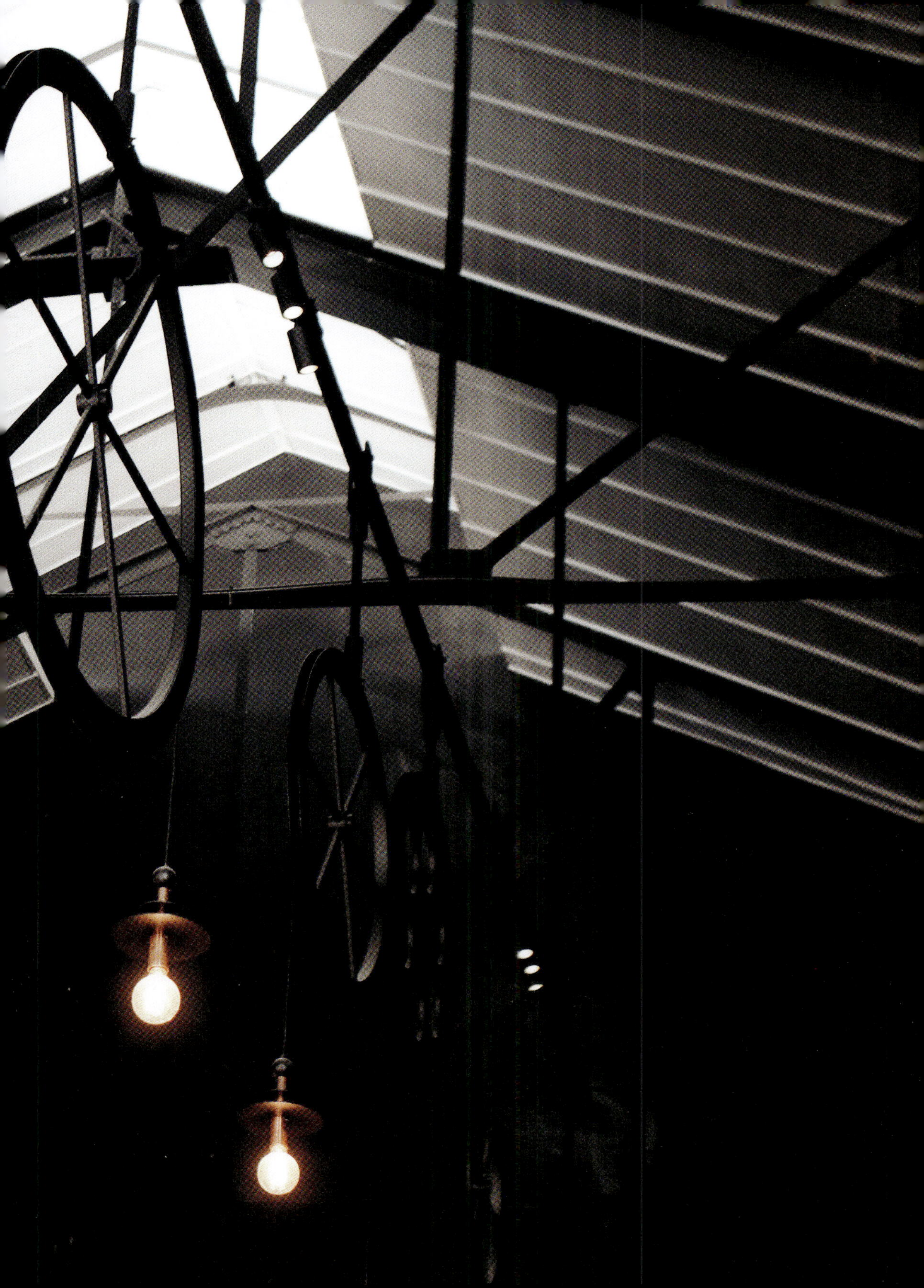

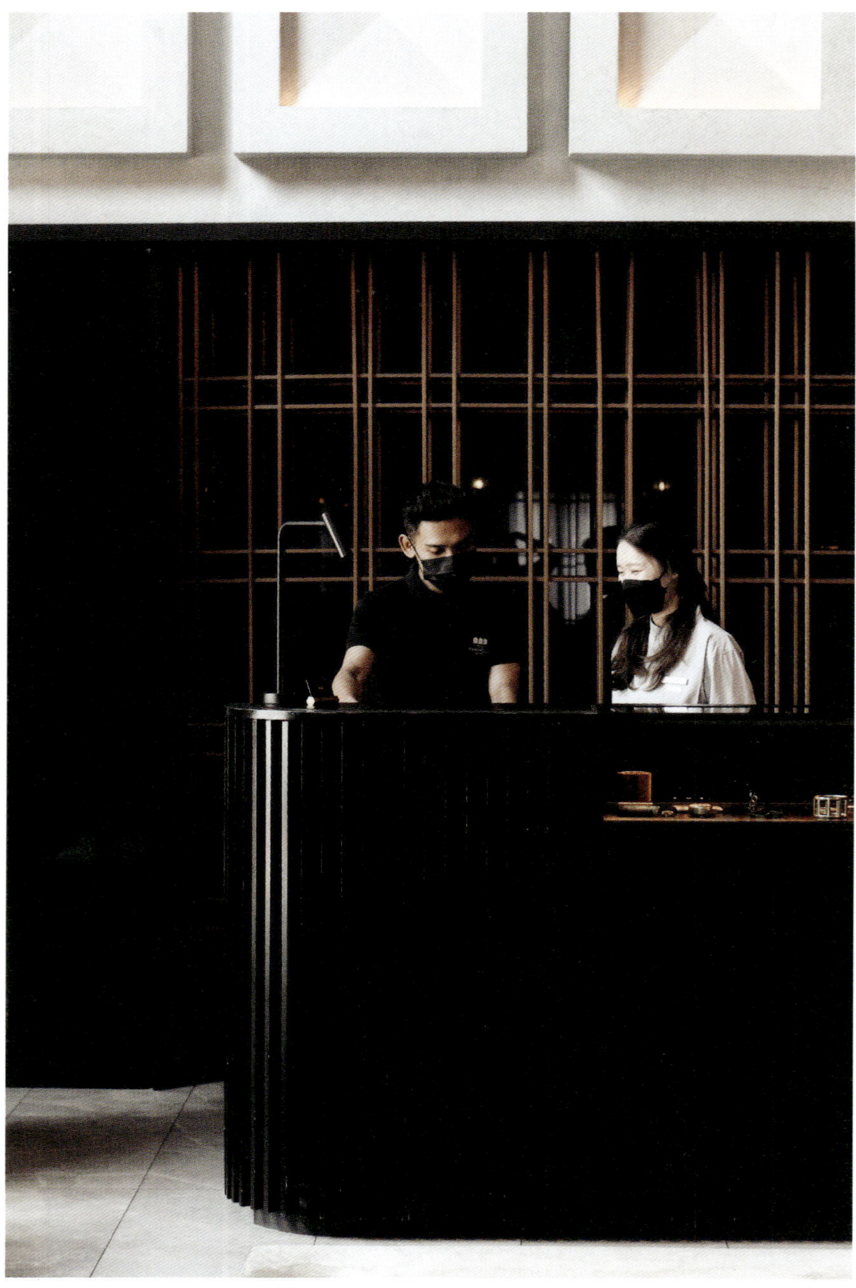

Check-in at The Warehouse Hotel                    Thursday 12:15 PM

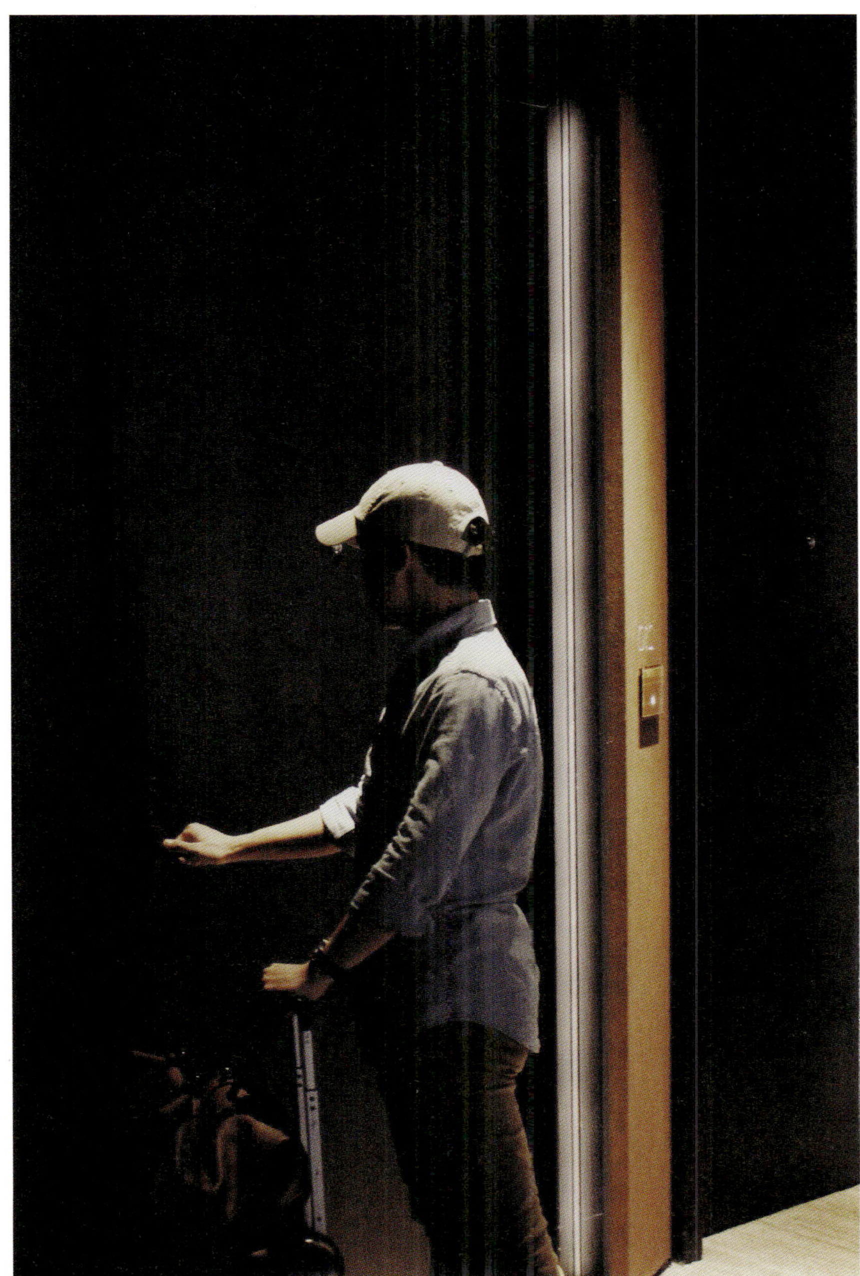

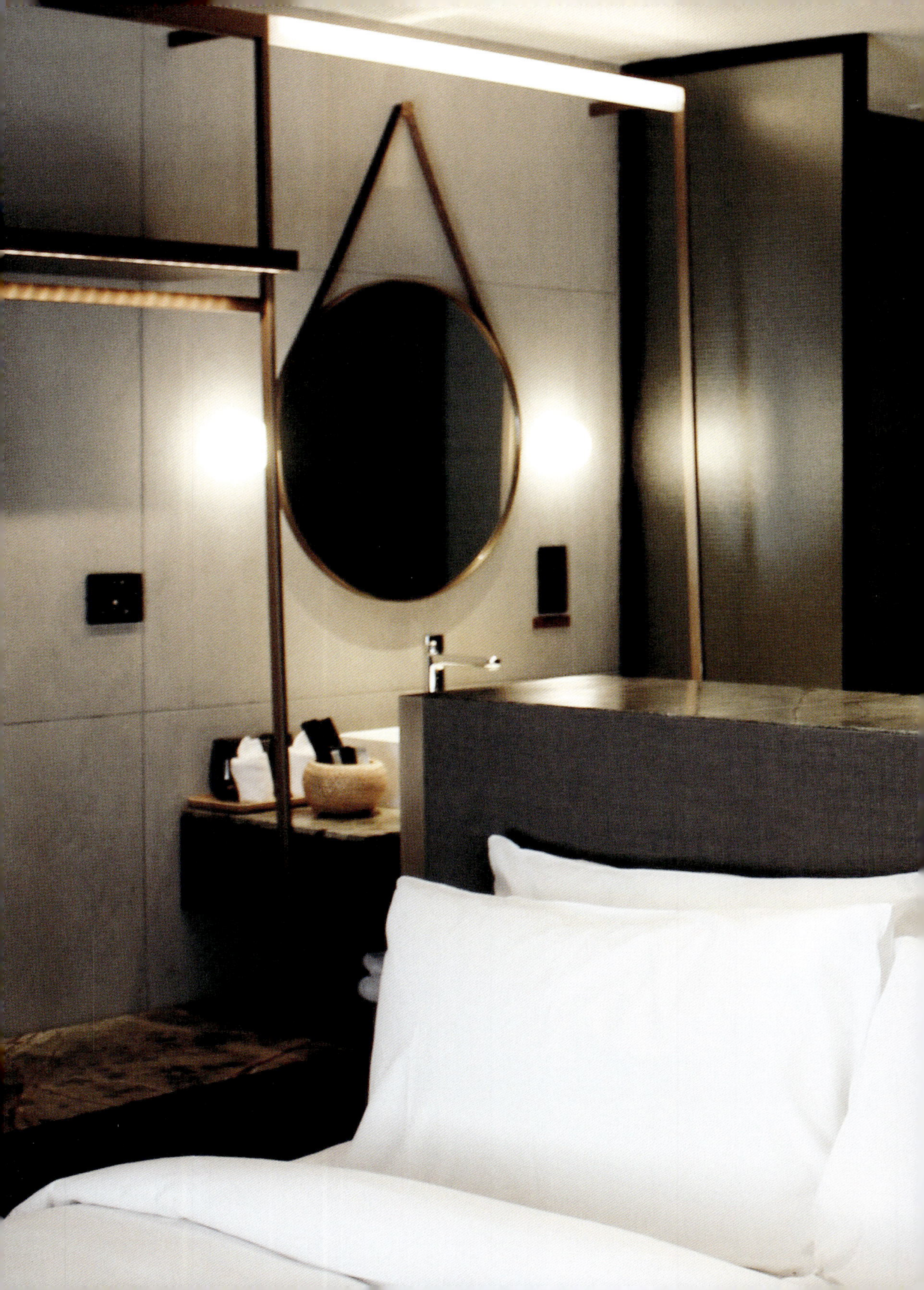

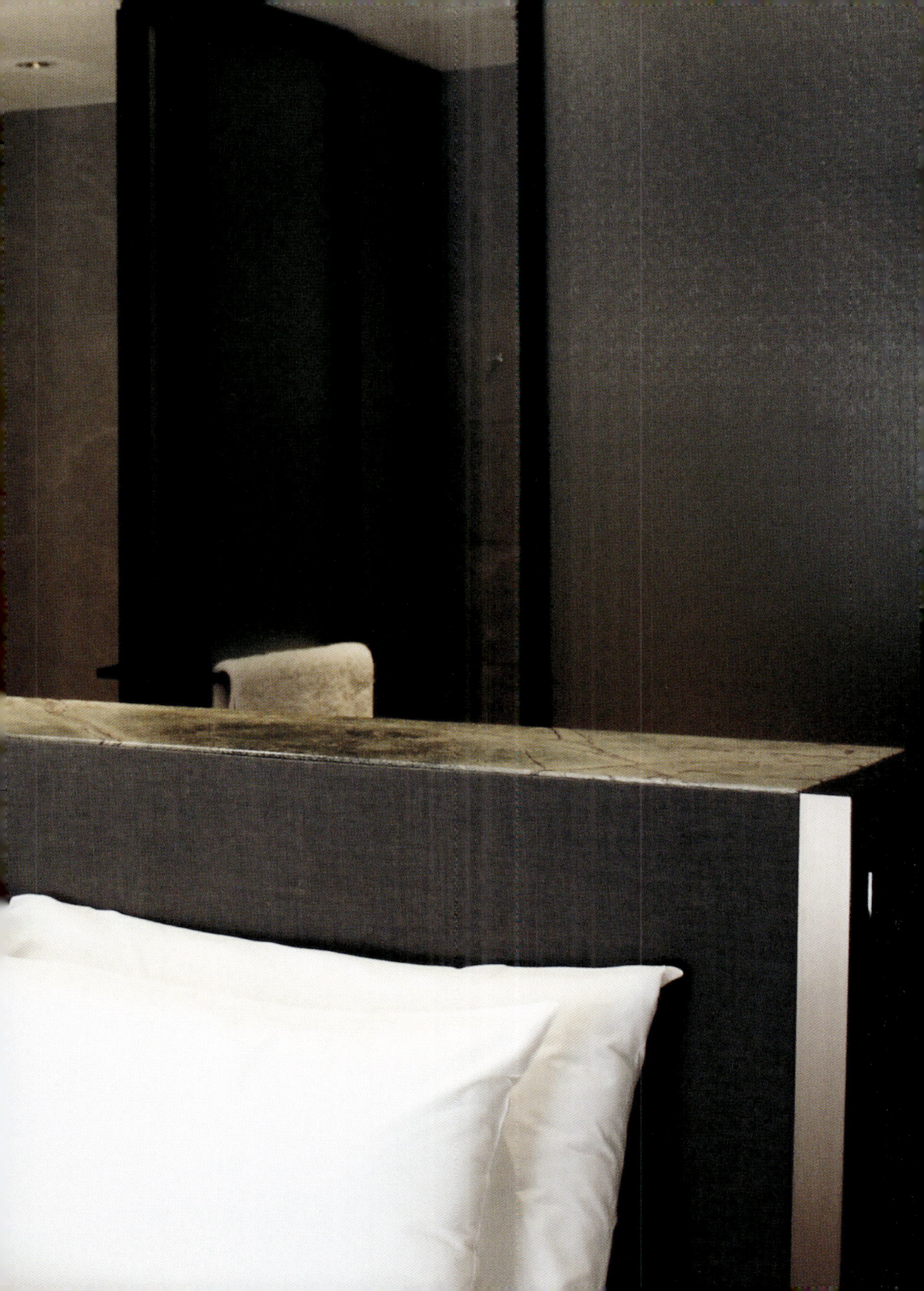

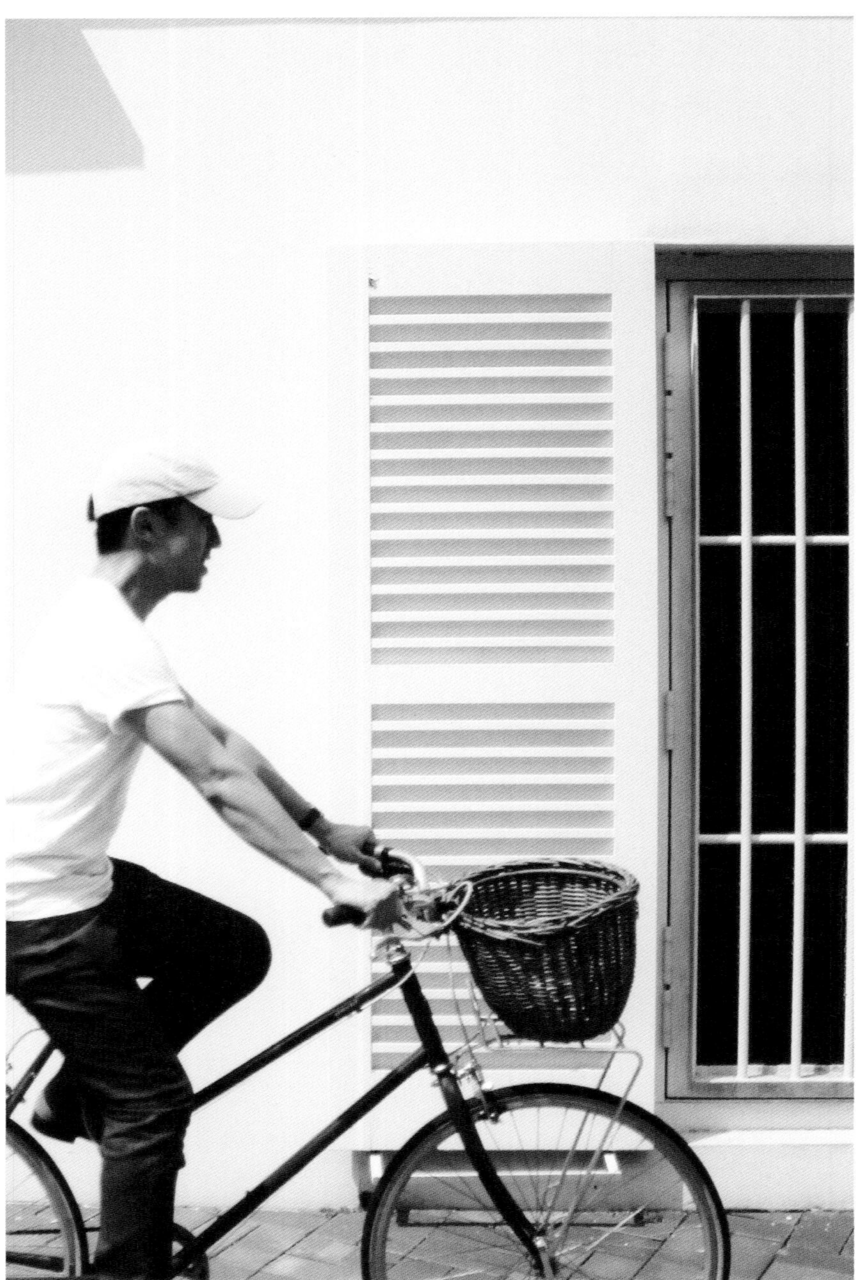

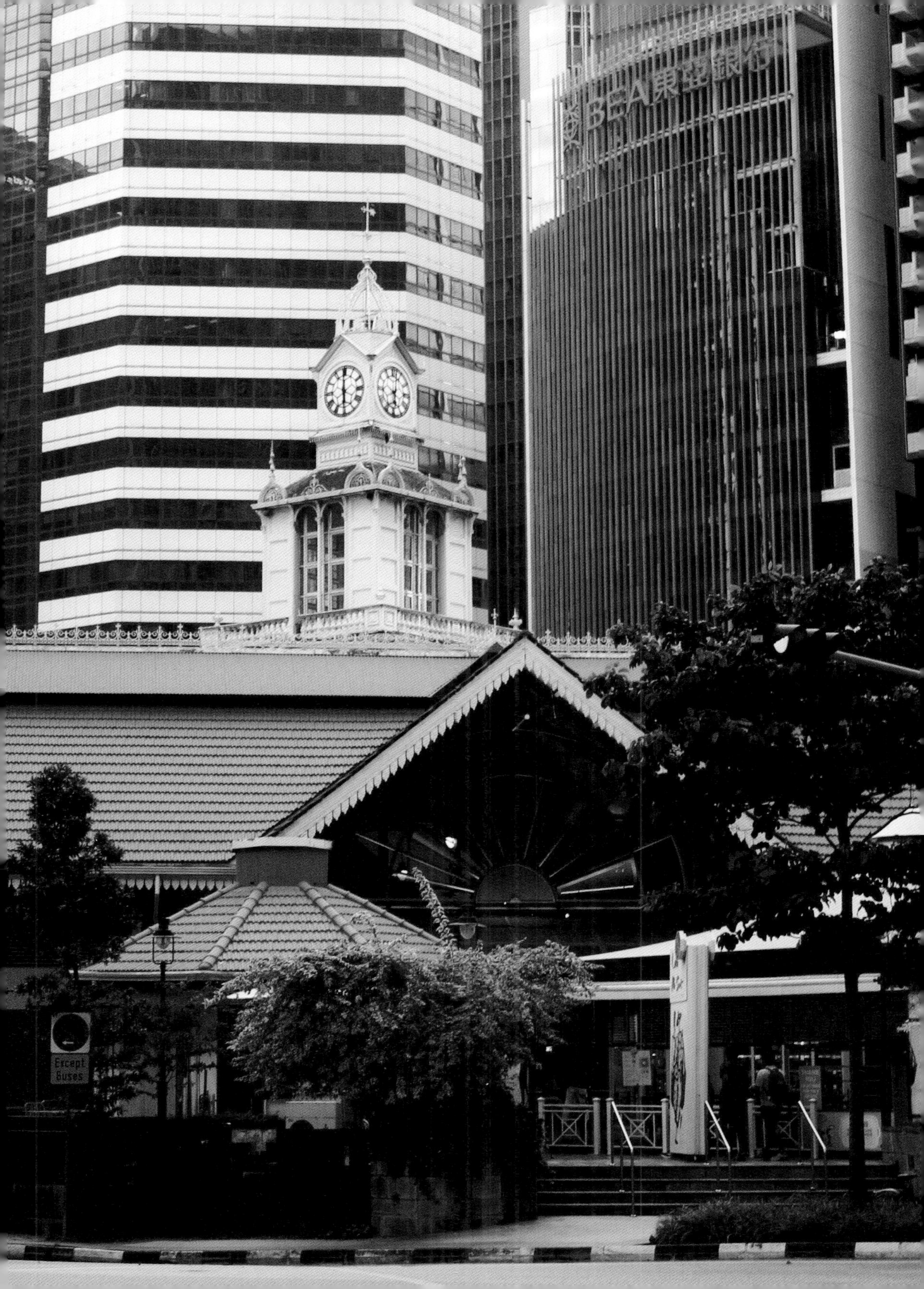

BEA 東亞銀行
Except Buses

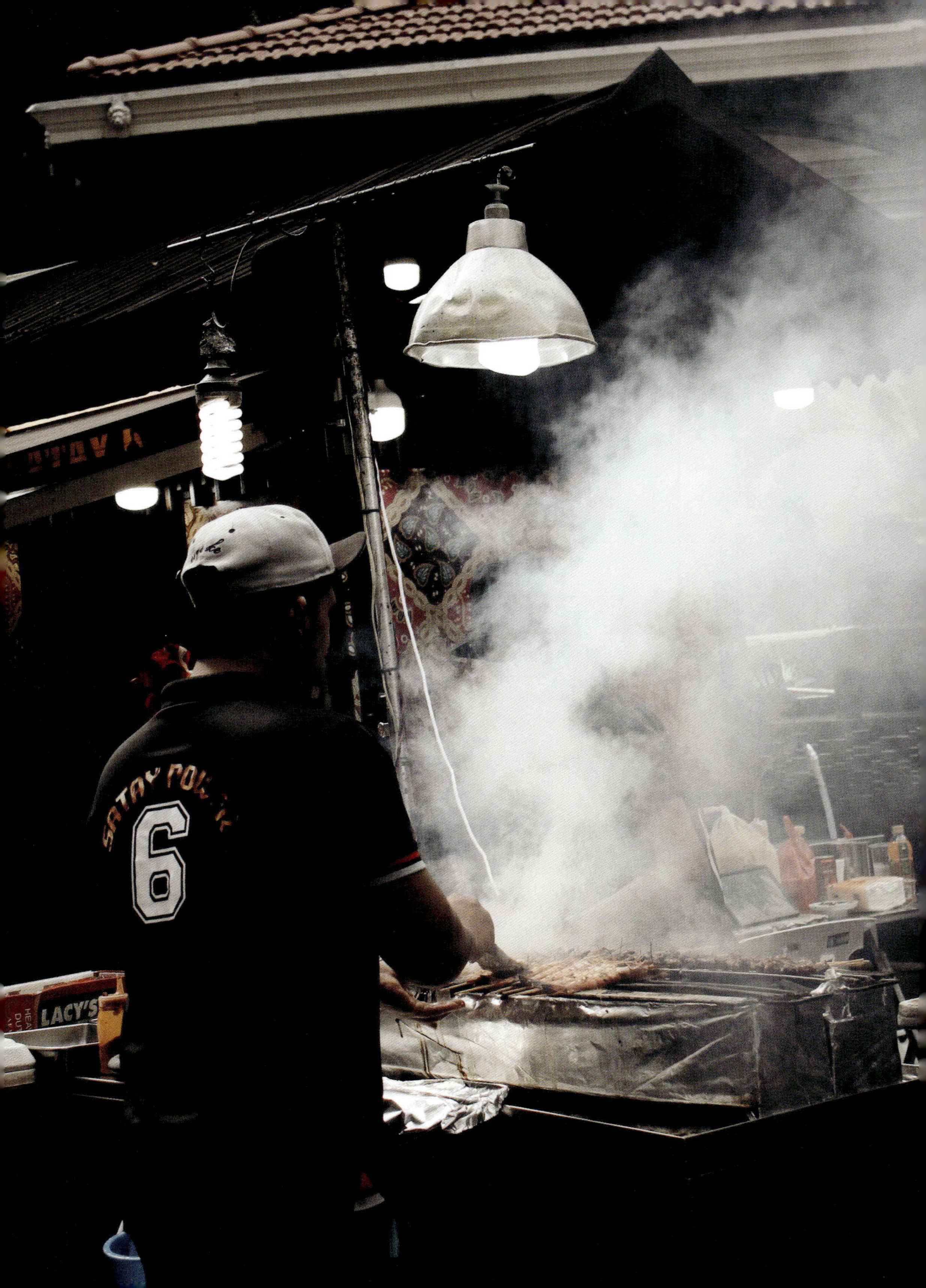

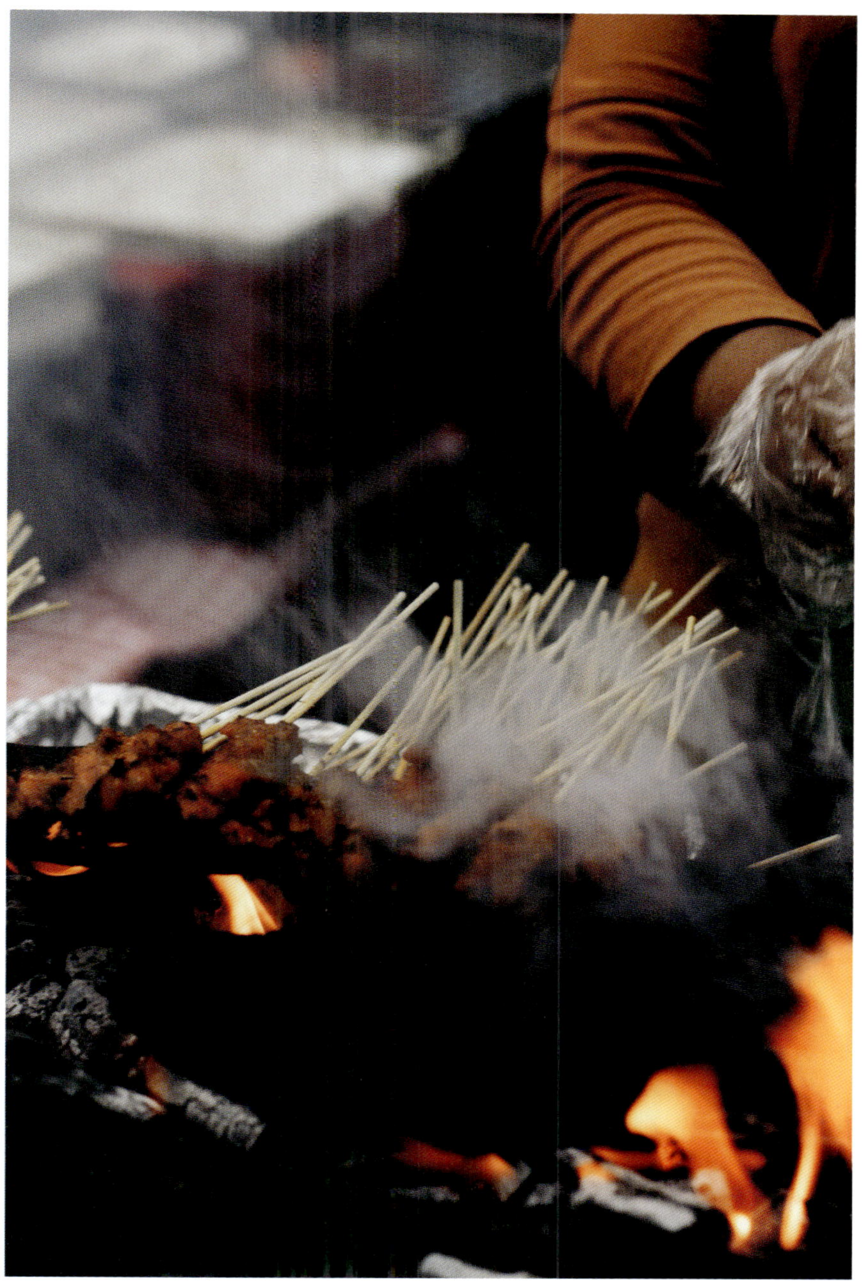



Lunch at Lau Pa Sat

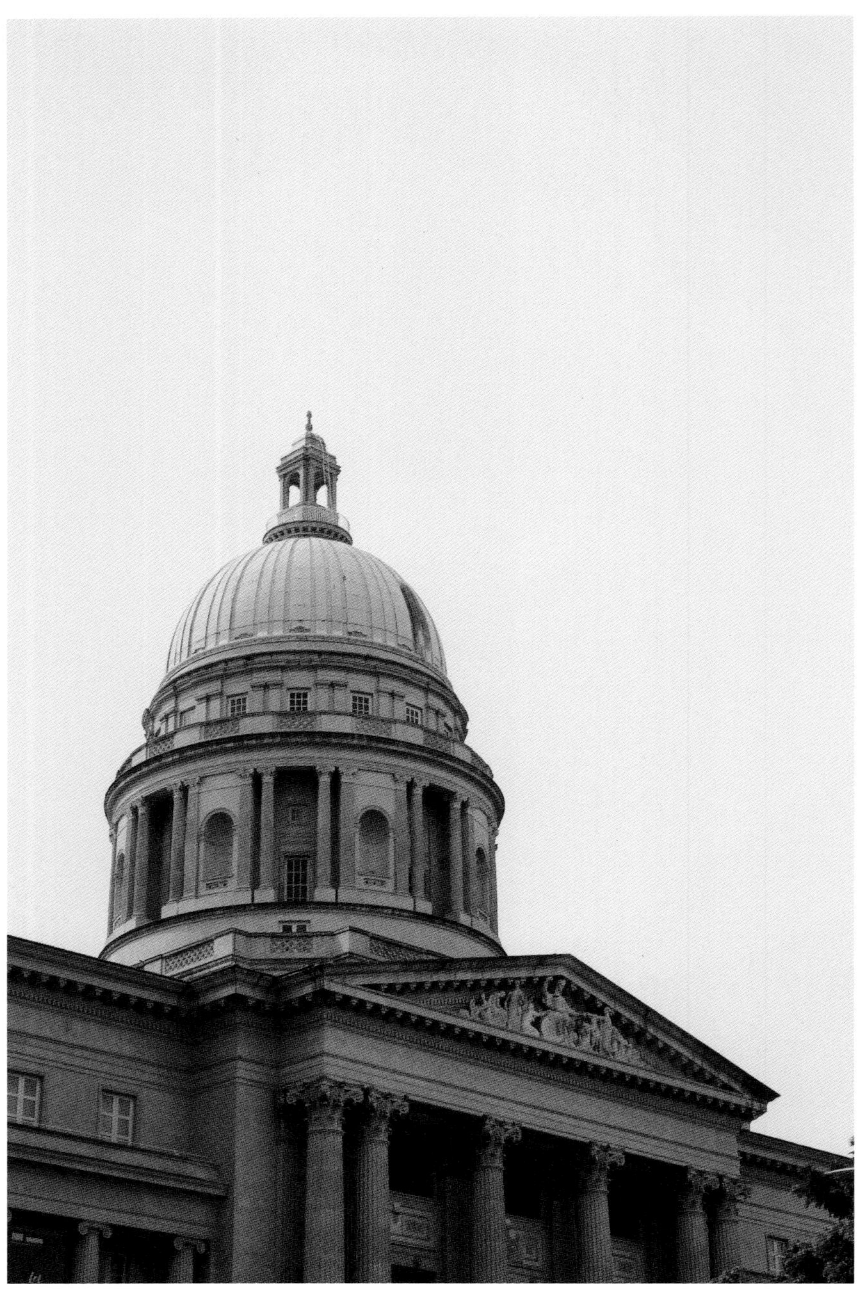

National Gallery Singapore

Thursday 3:35 PM

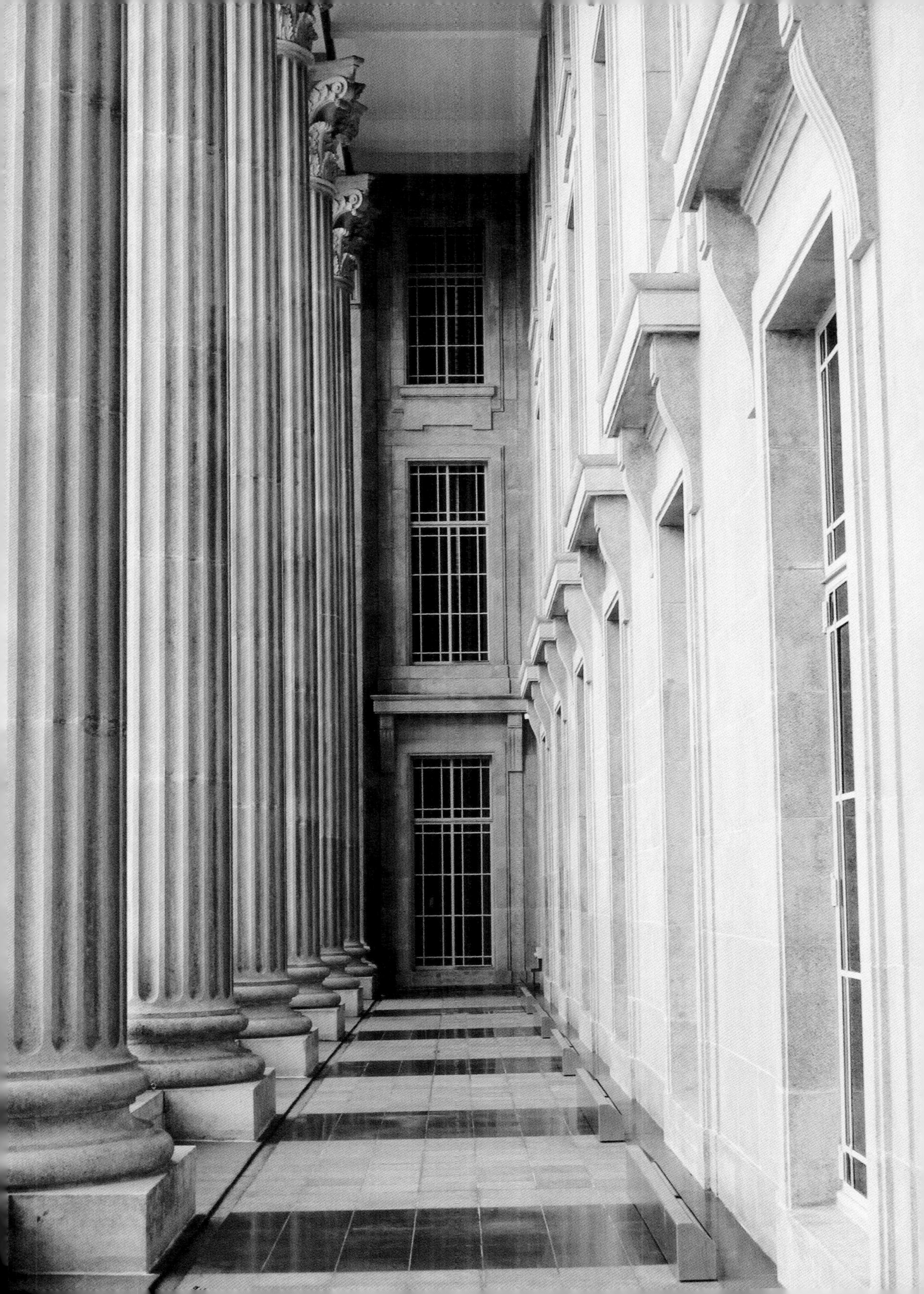

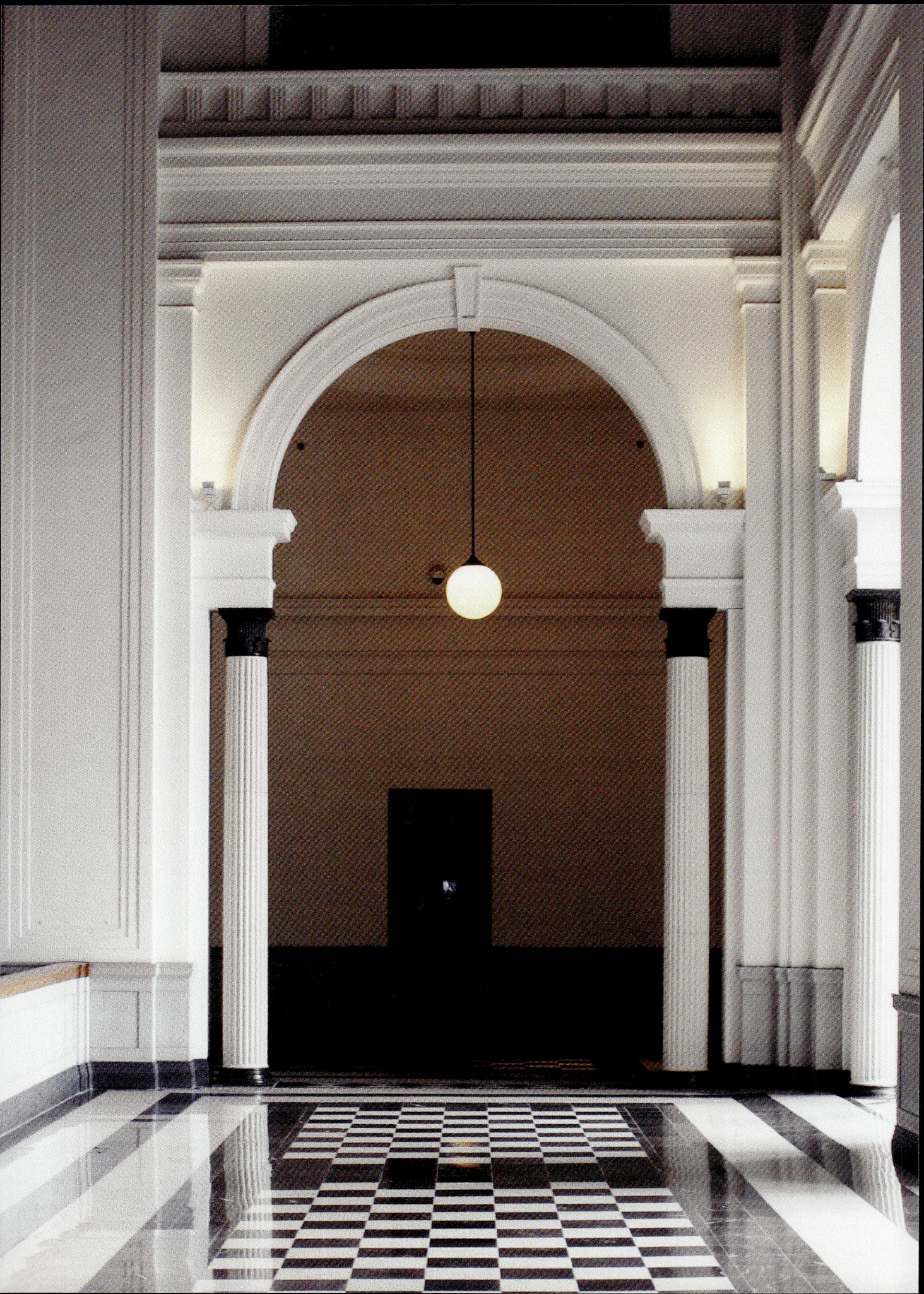

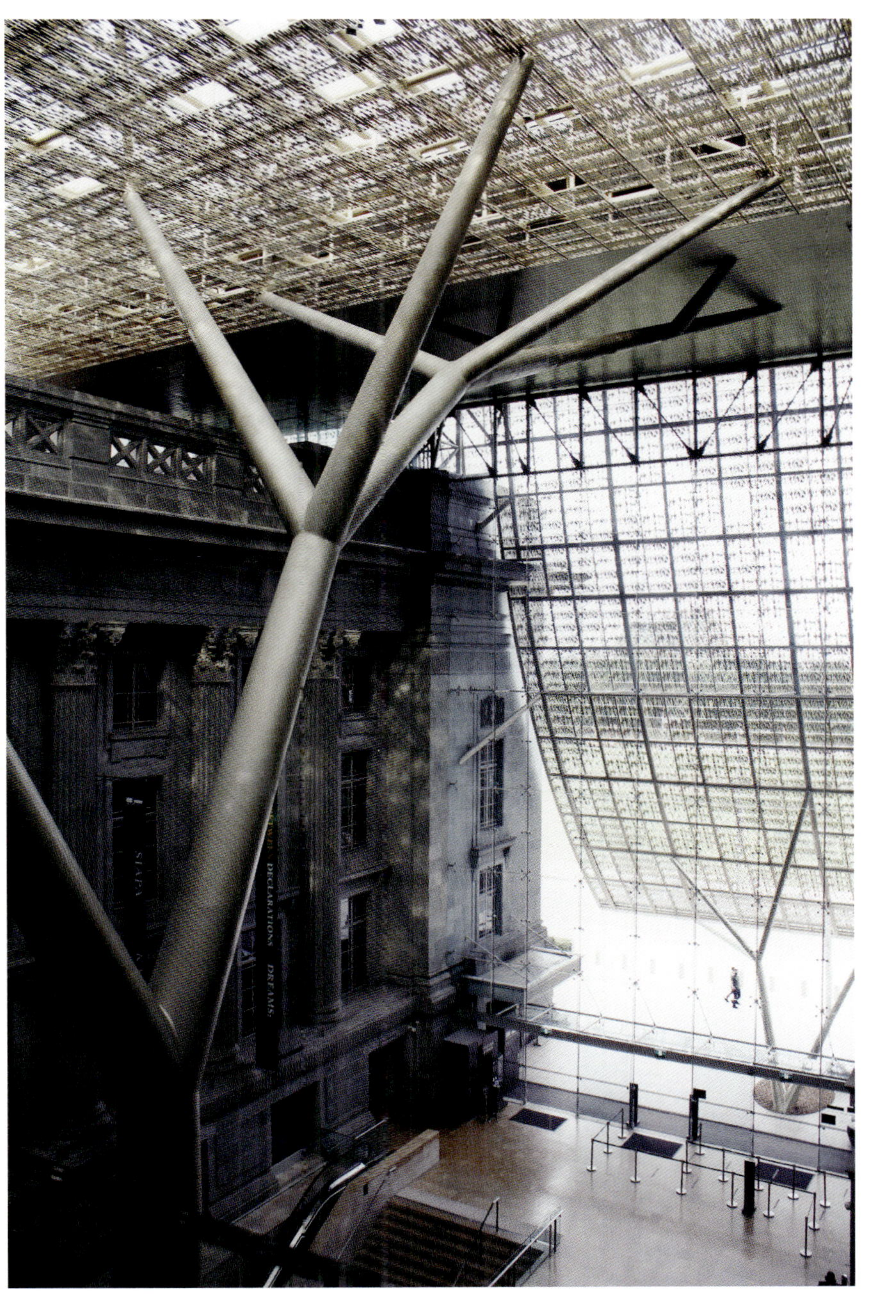

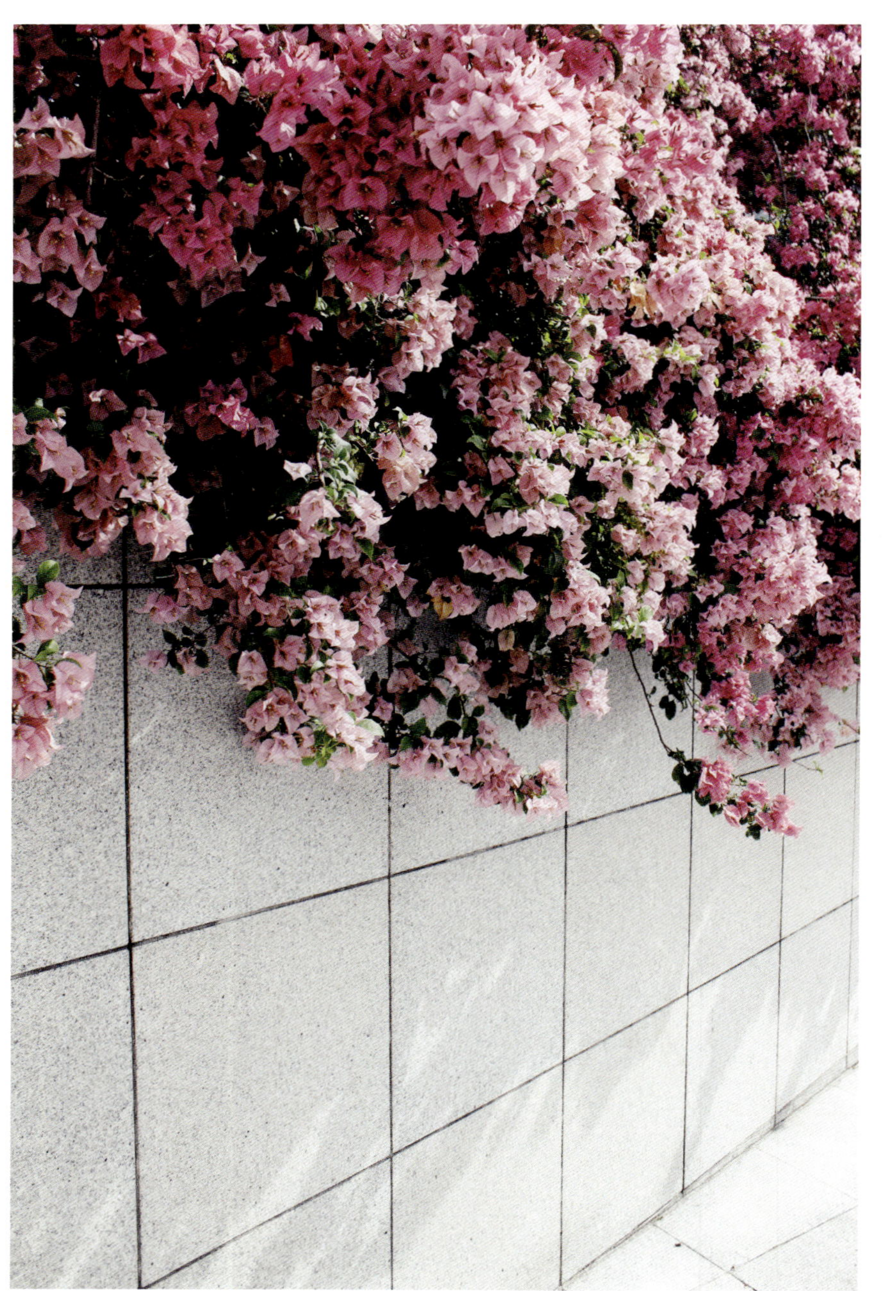

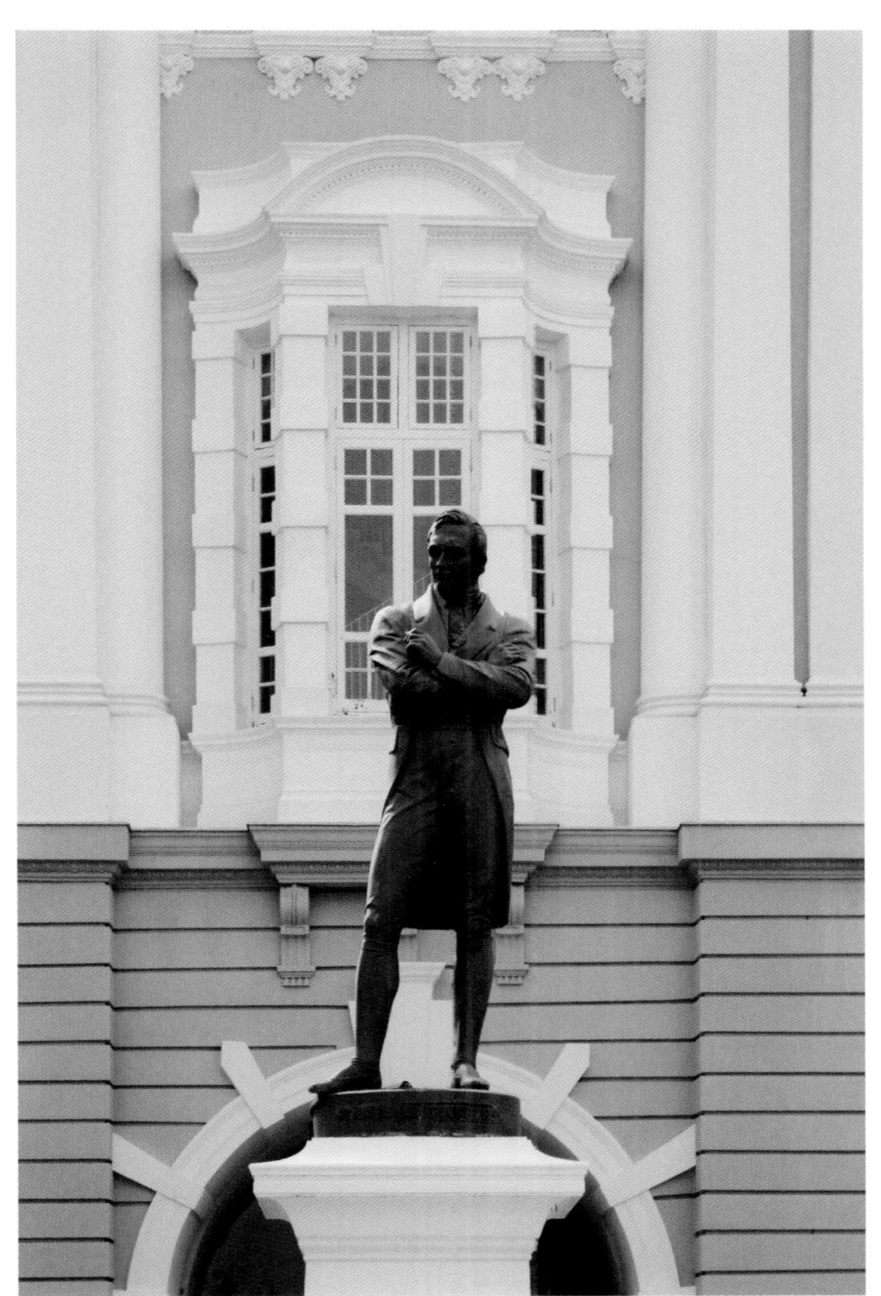

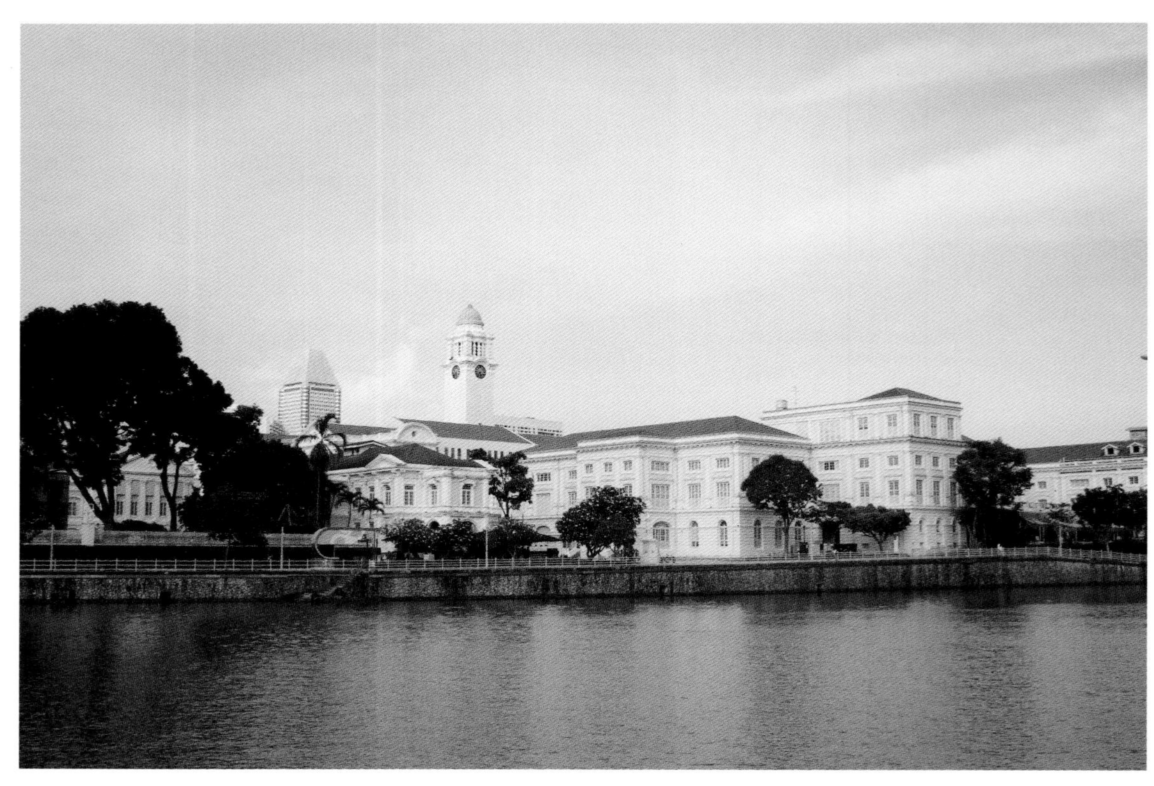

Enjoying old and new architecture                    Thursday 5:50 PM

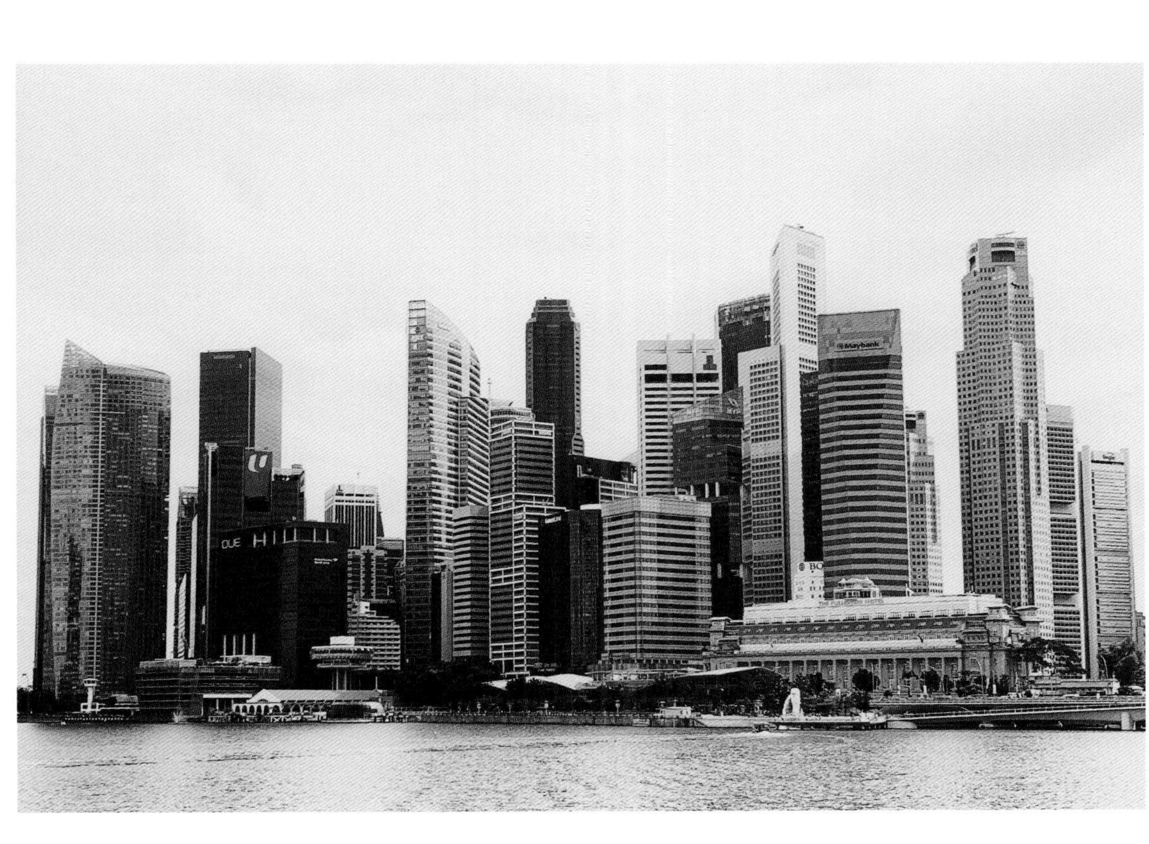

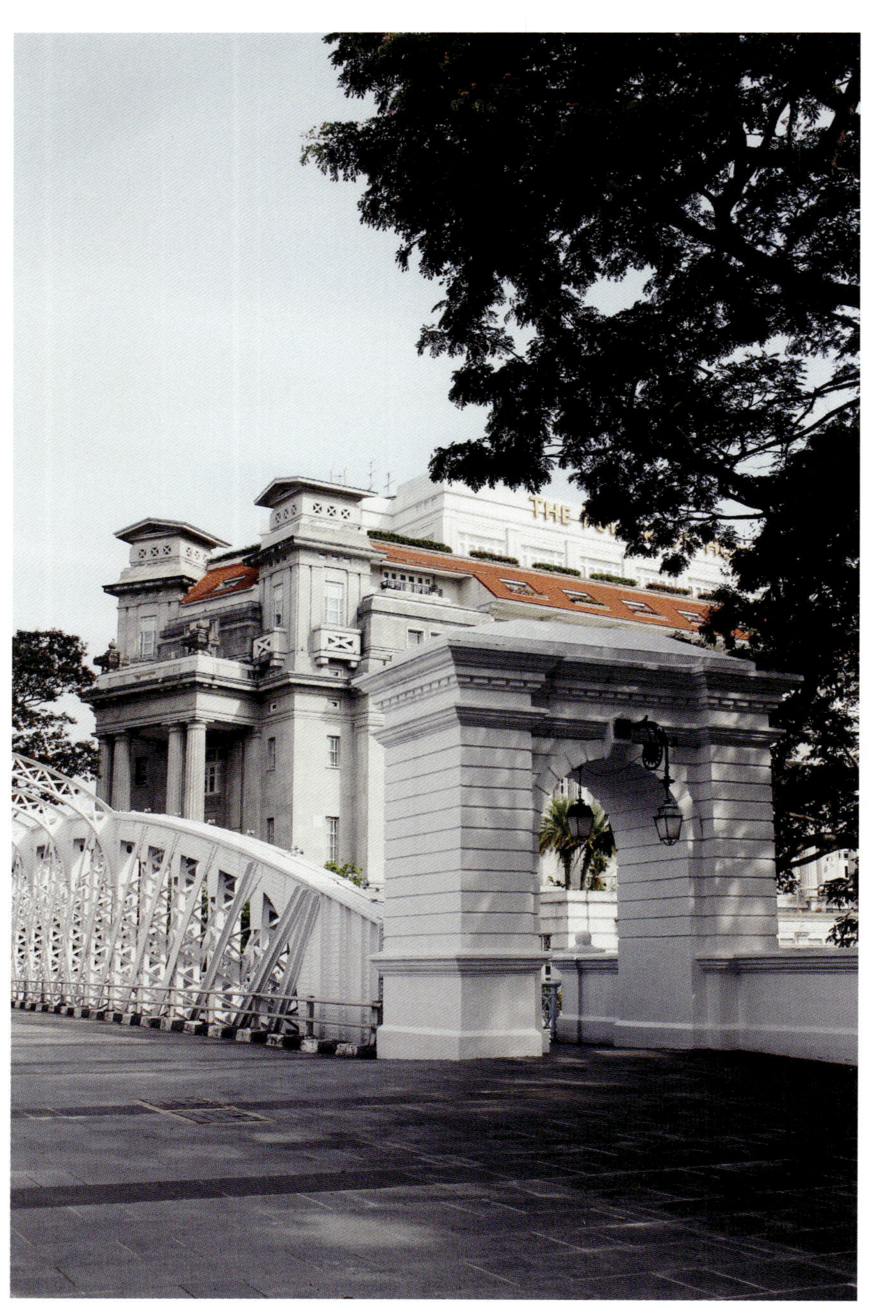

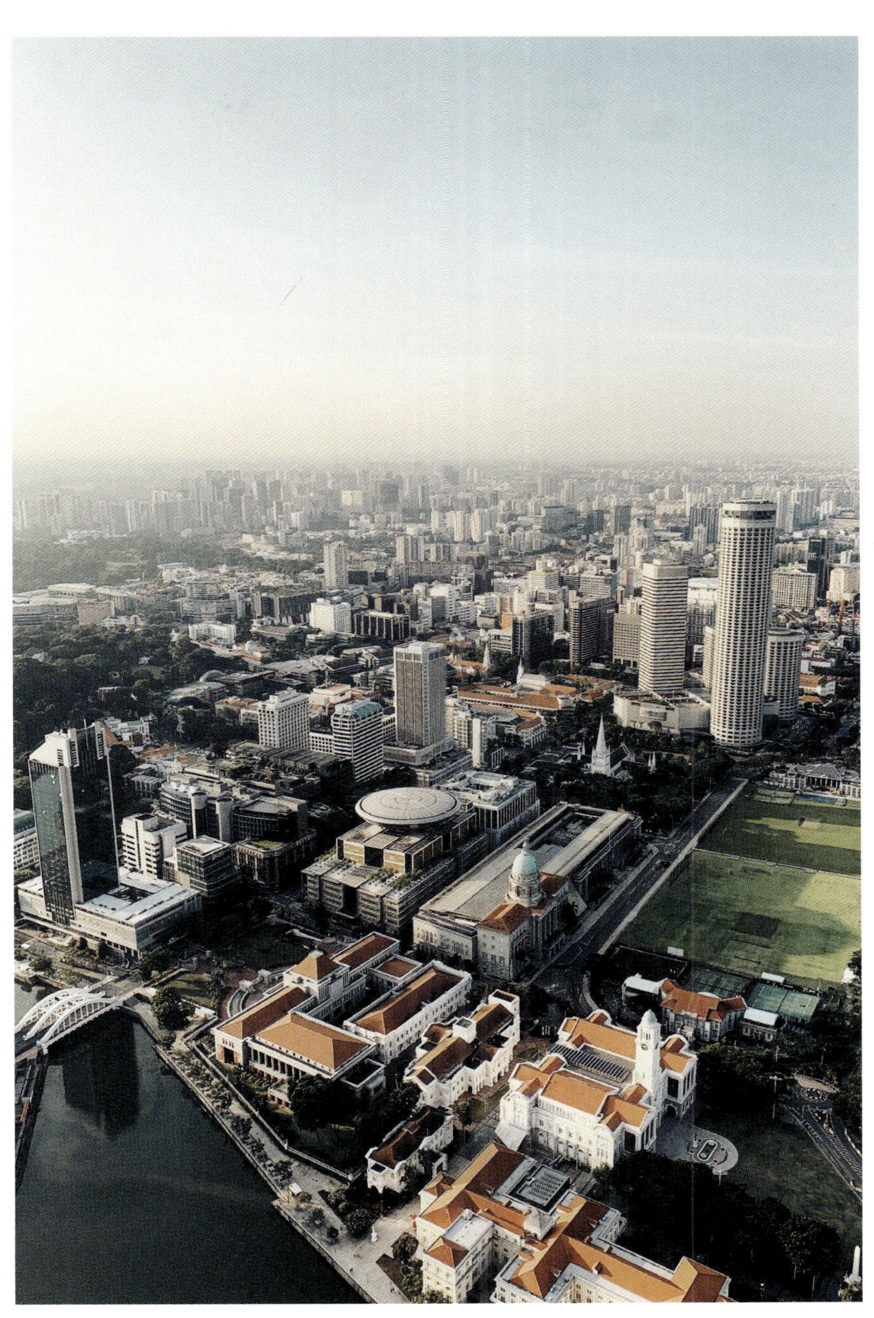

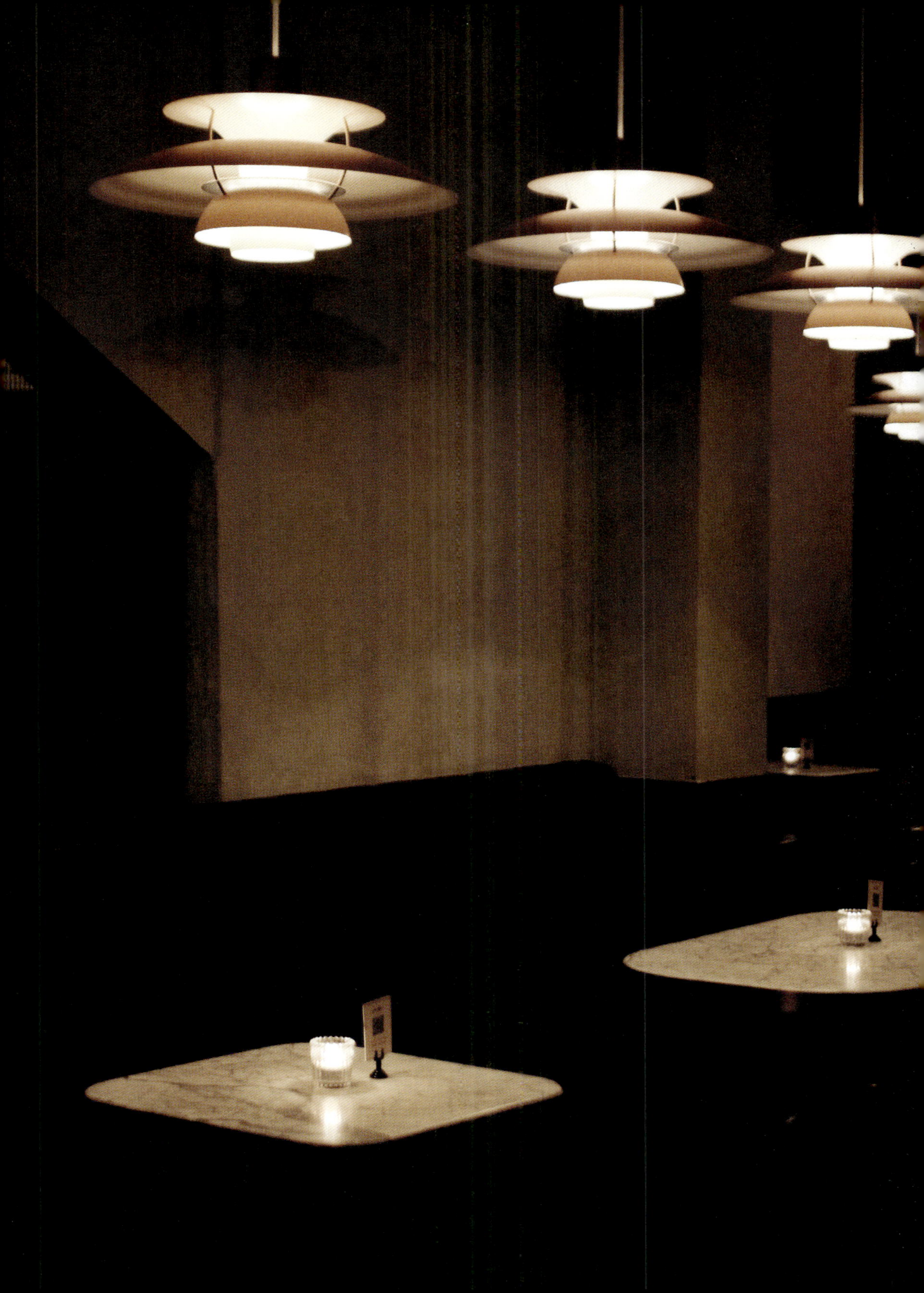

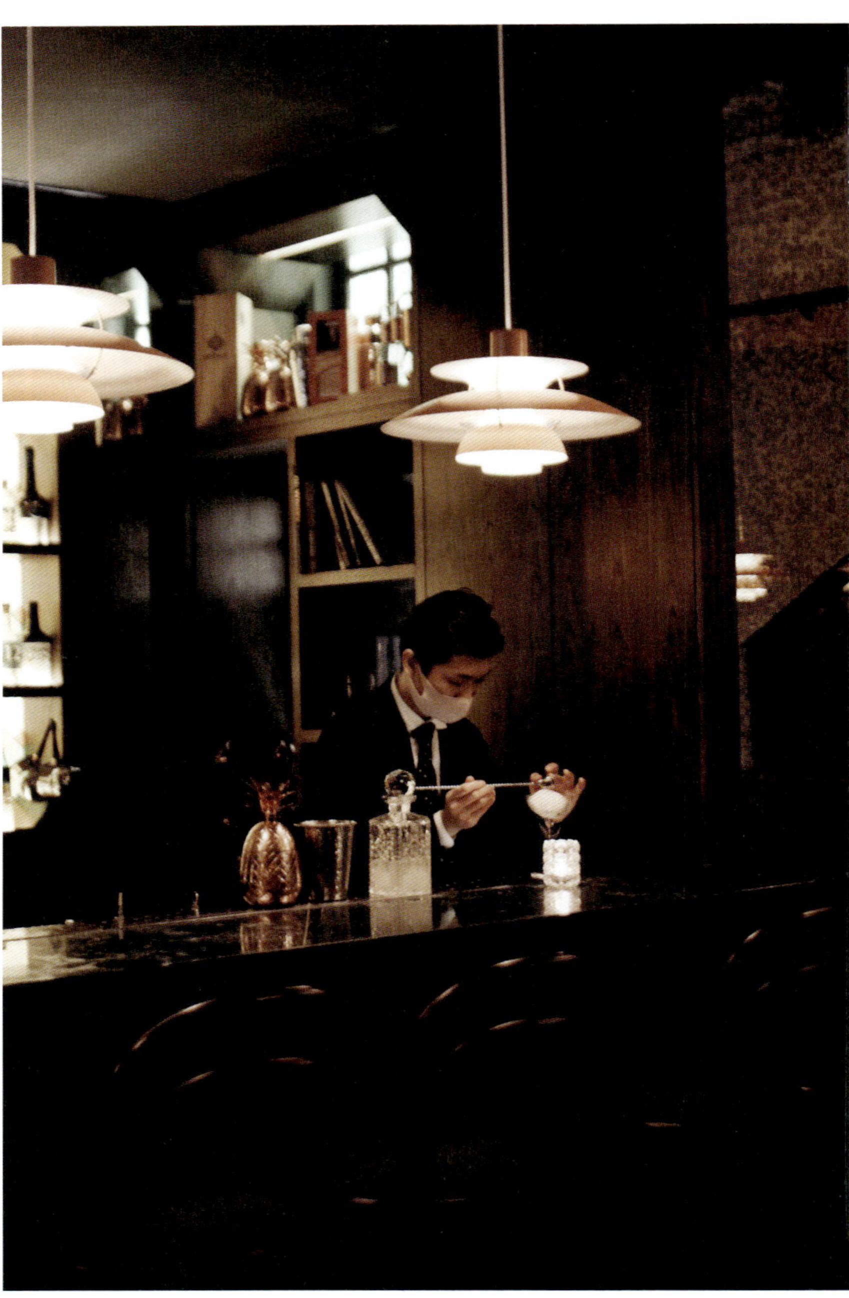

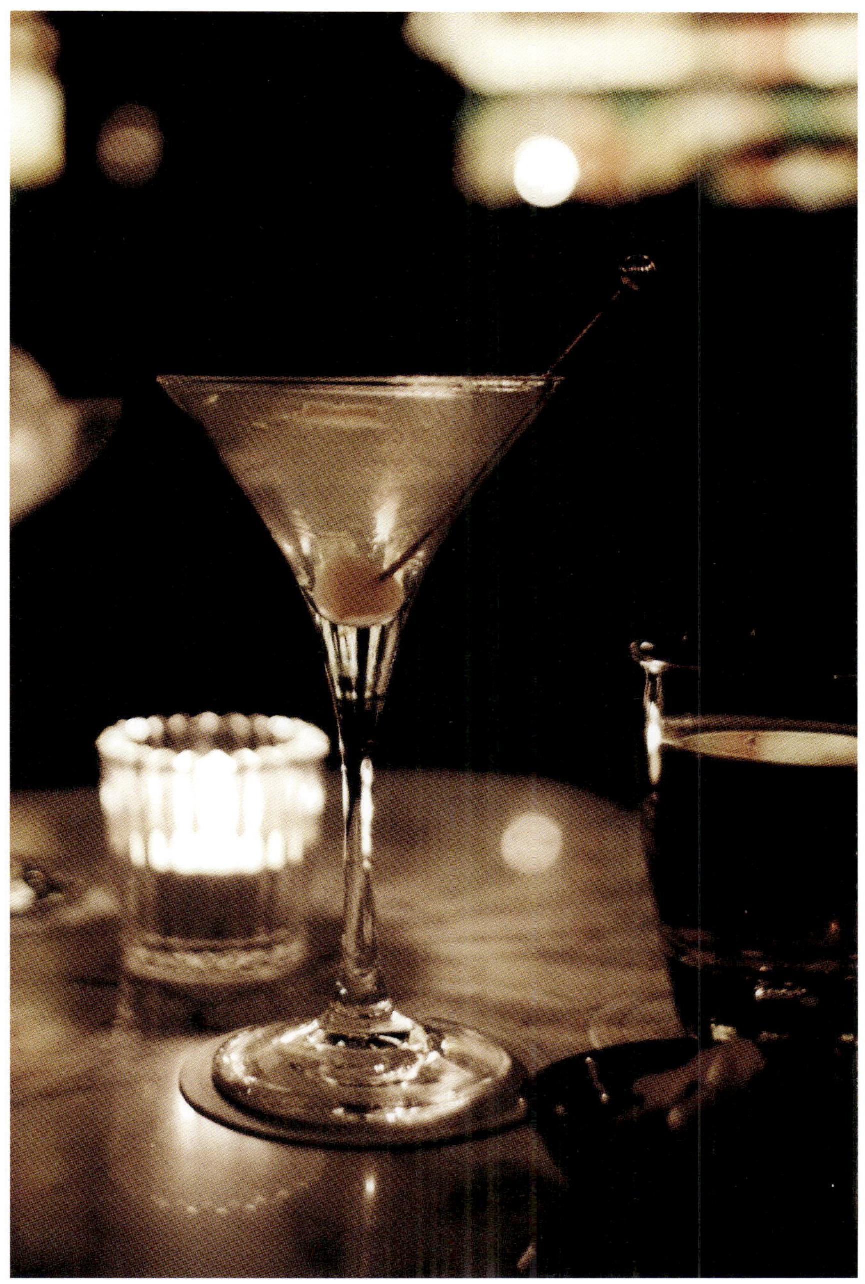

Thursday 8:00 PM                                    Cocktail at Gibson Bar

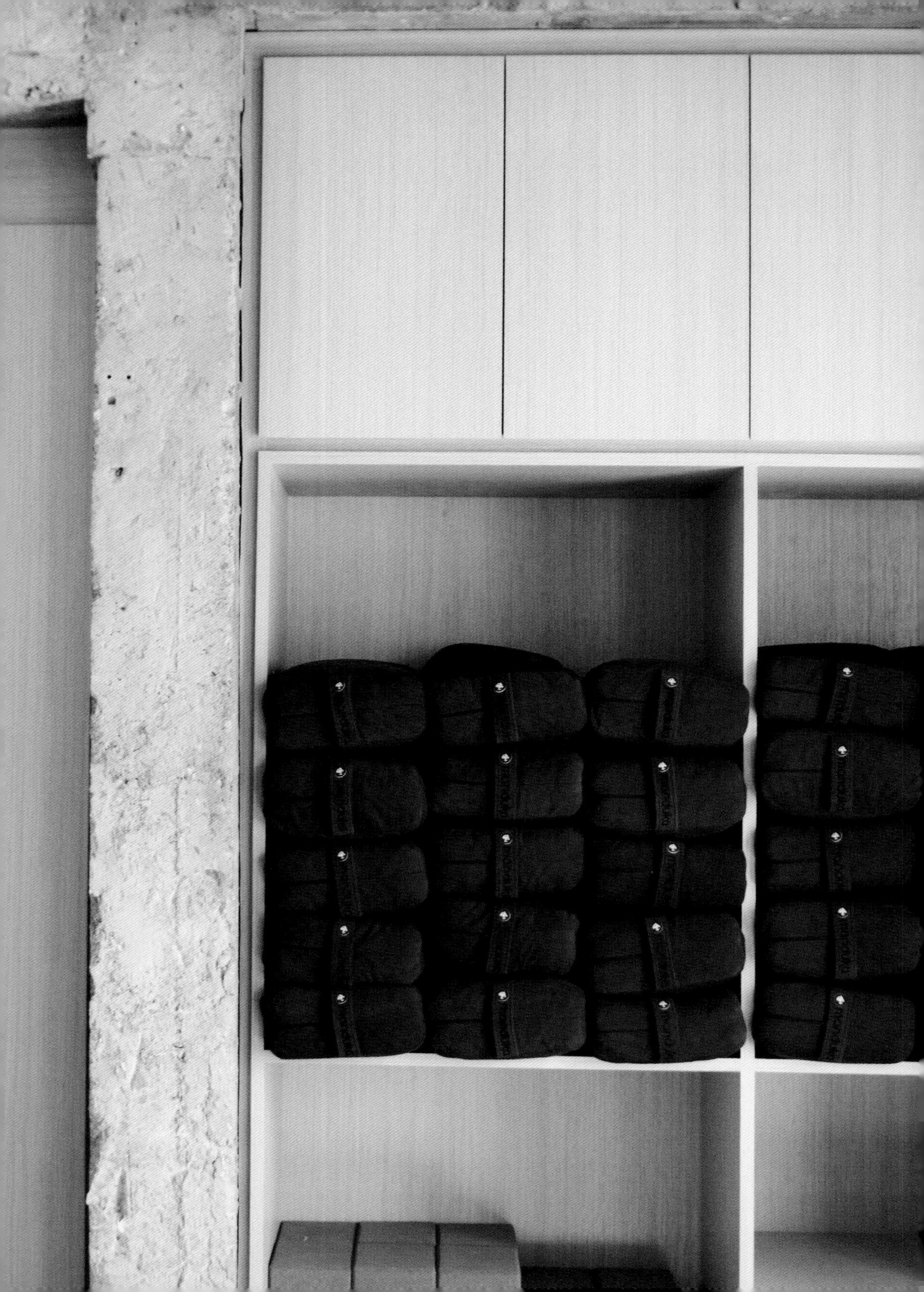

**Friday**

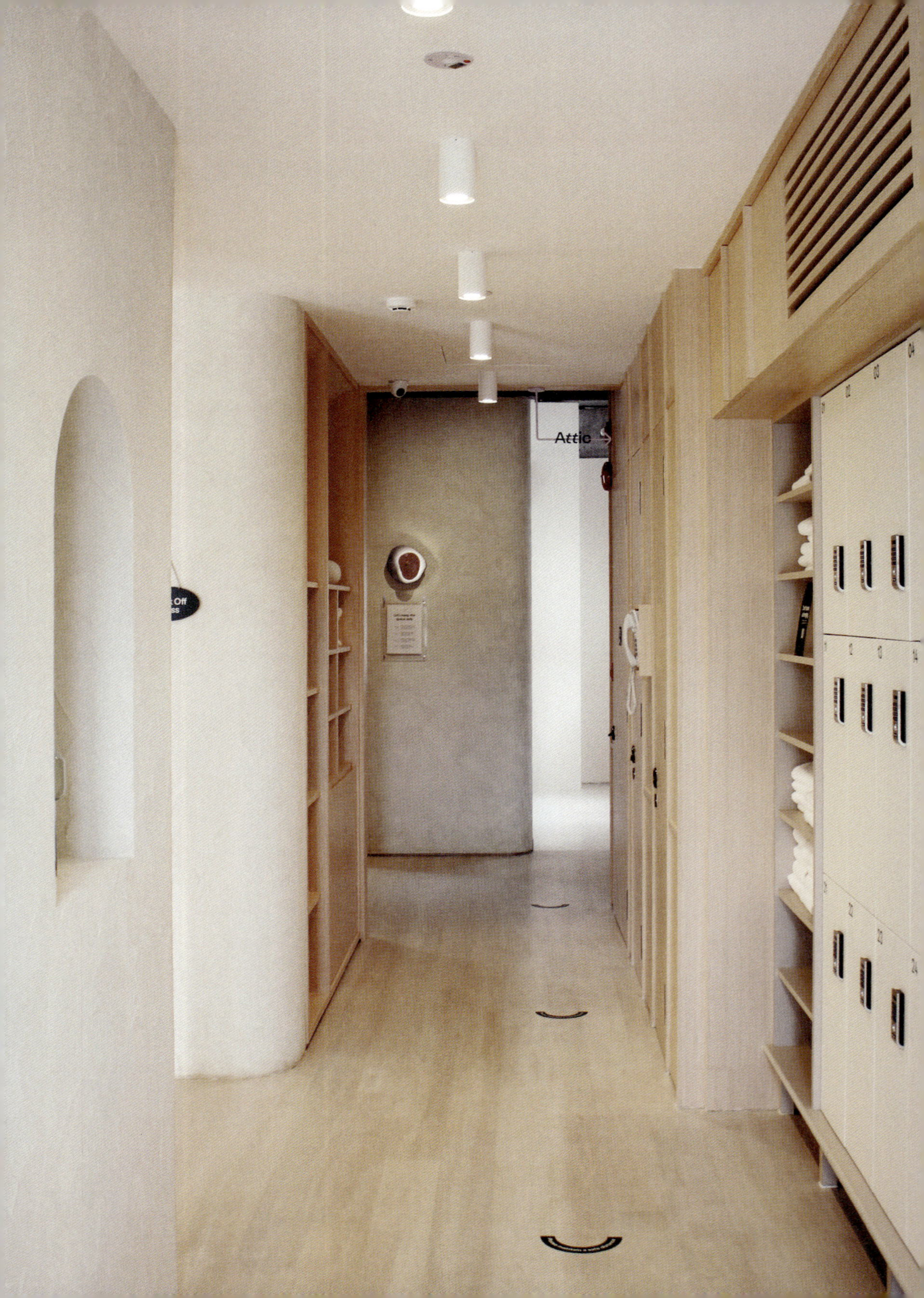
Off
ss
Attic

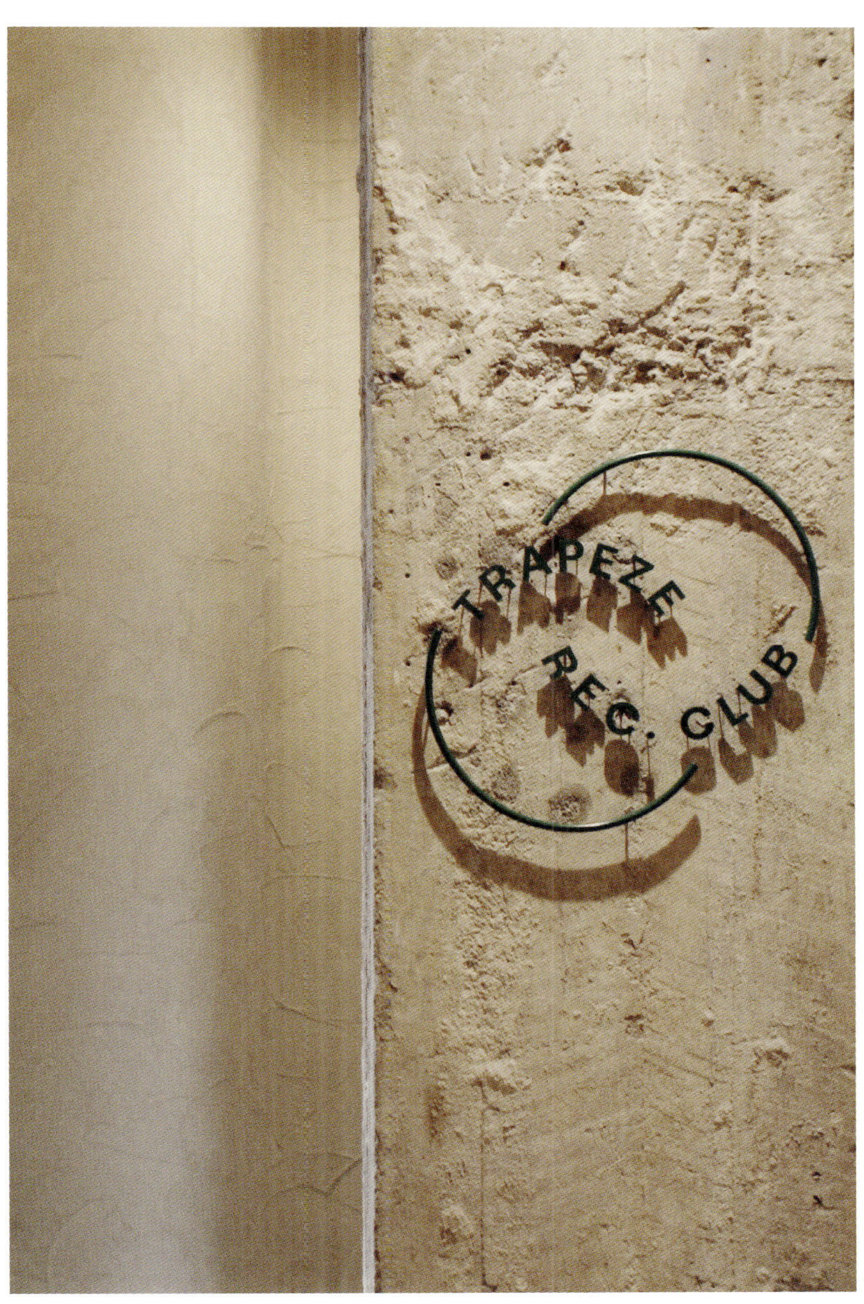



Friday 7:30 AM

Yoga at Trapeze Rec. Club

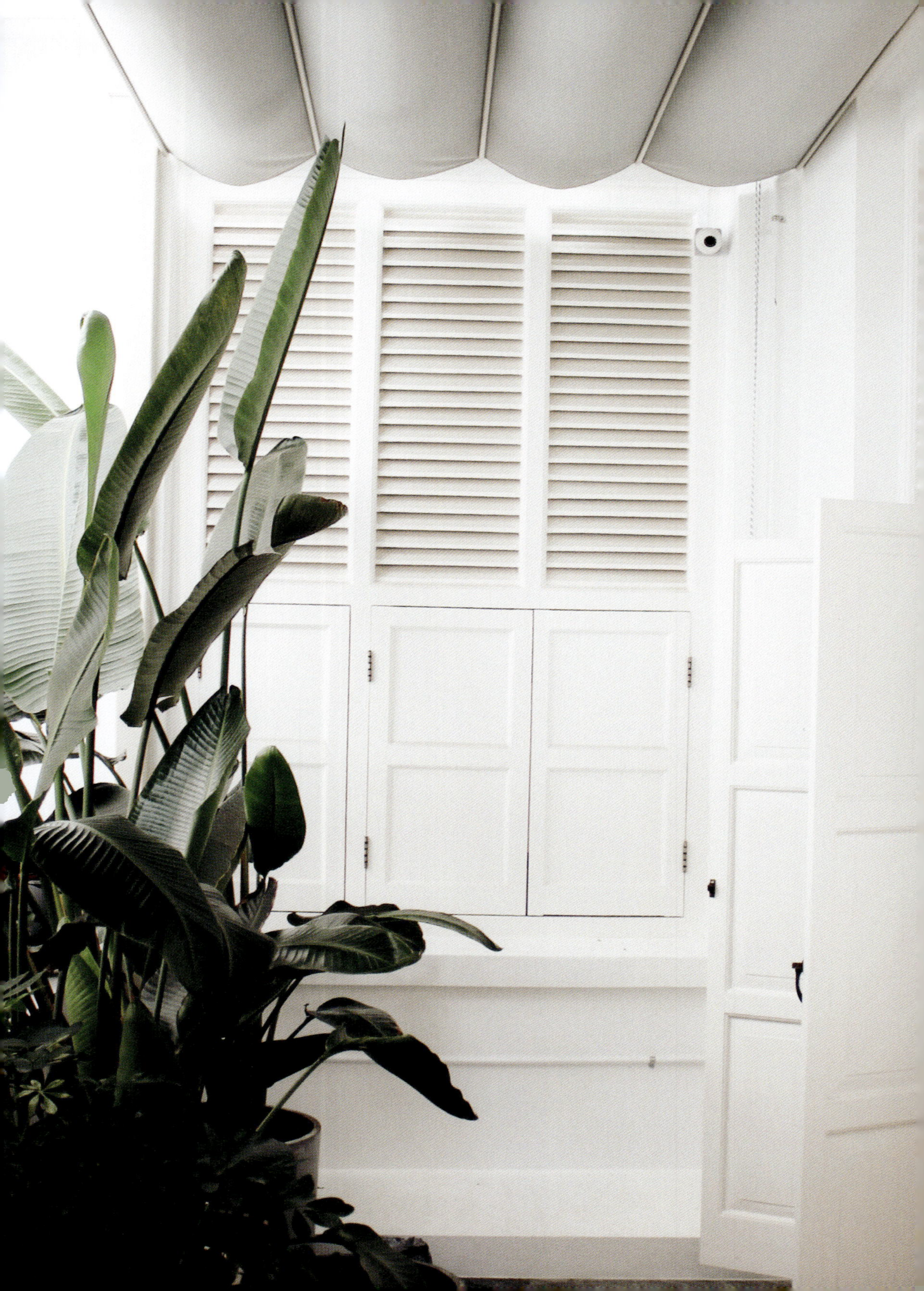

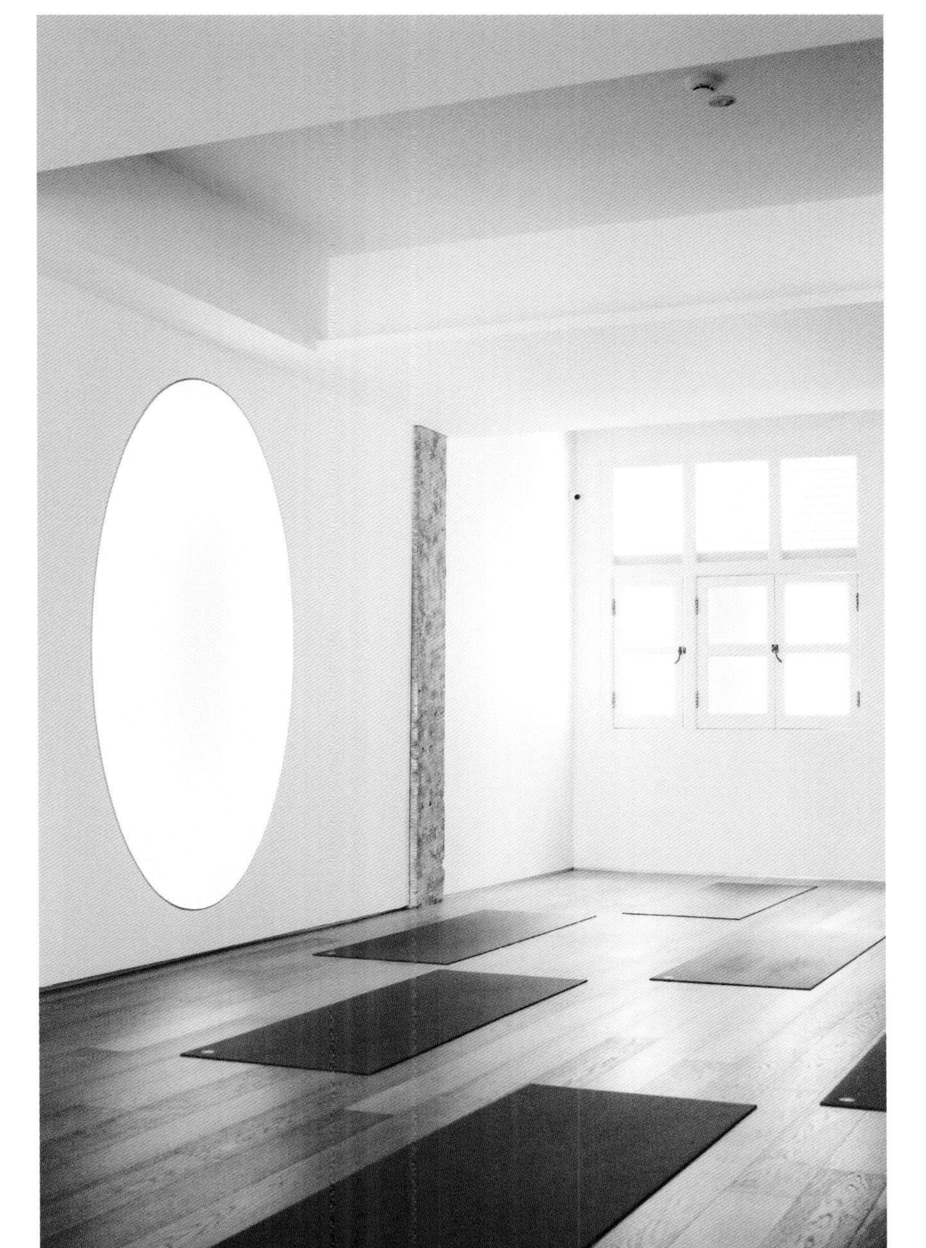

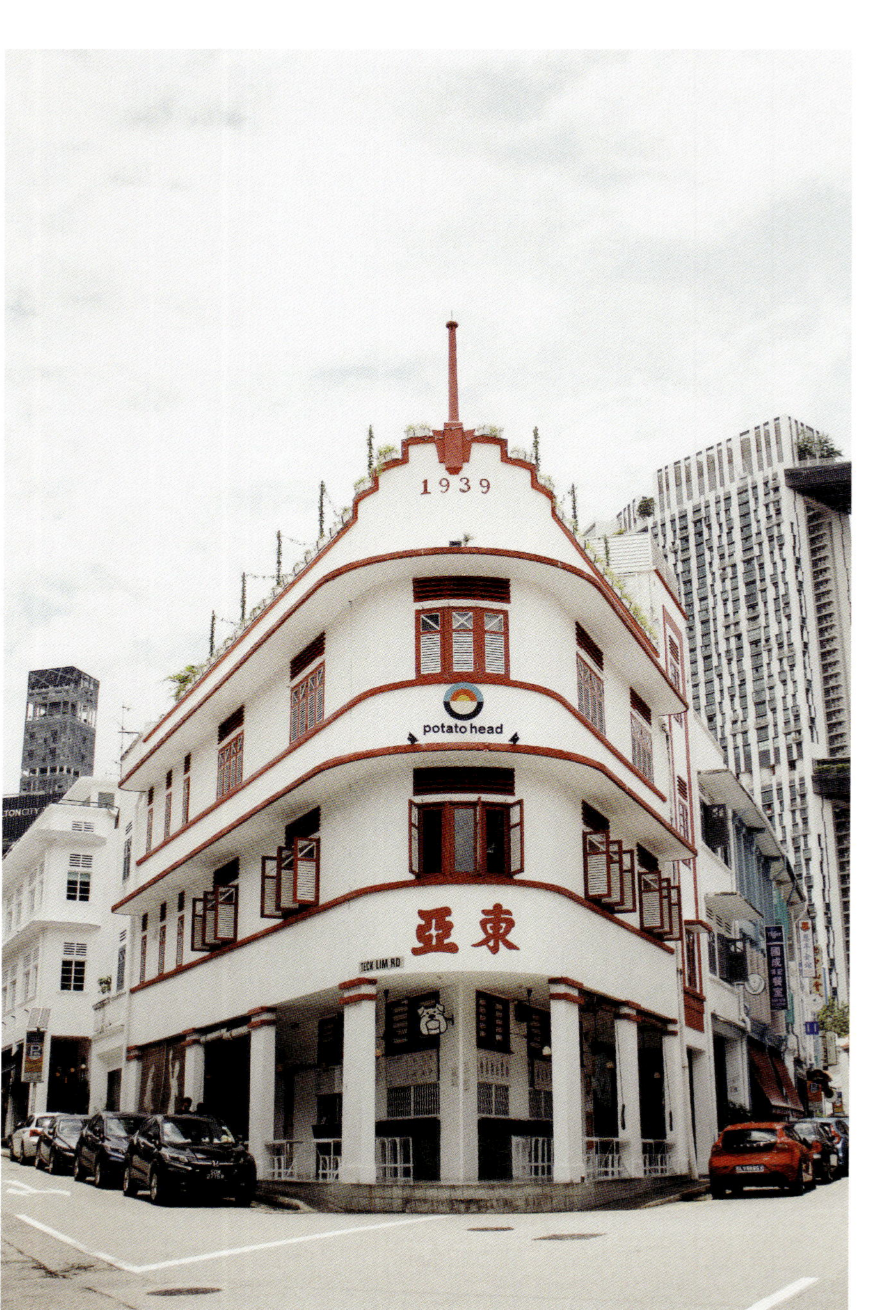

1939
potato head
東亞
TECK LIM RD

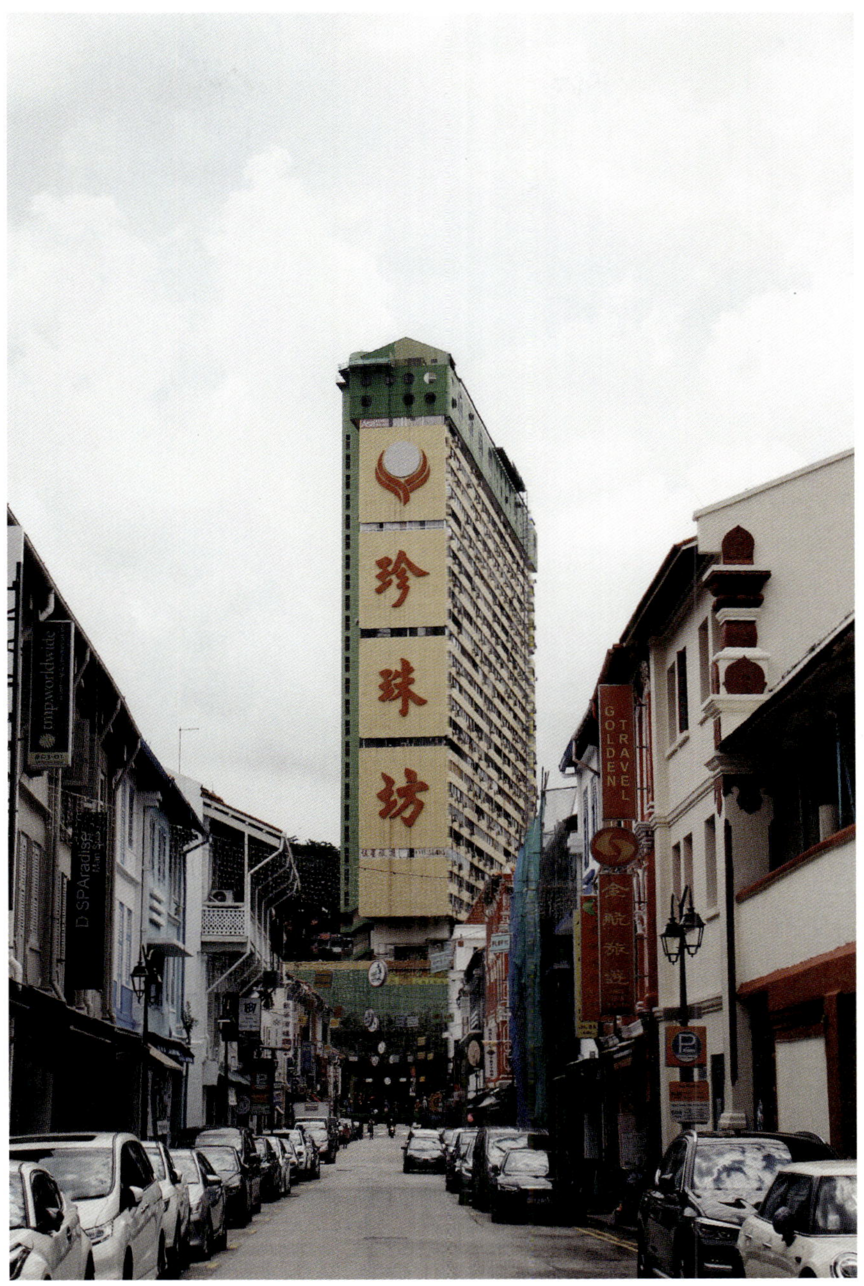




Walking through Chinatown

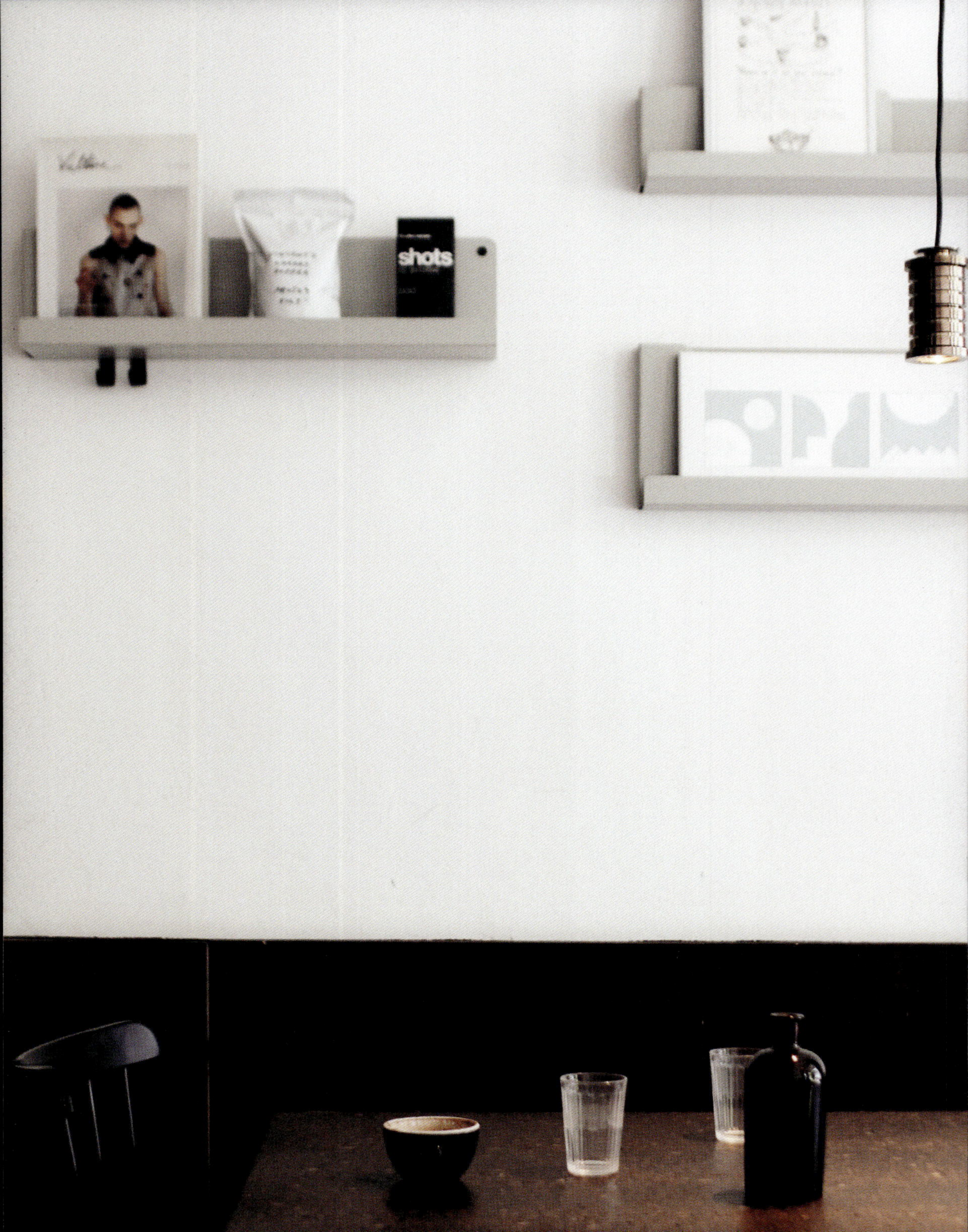

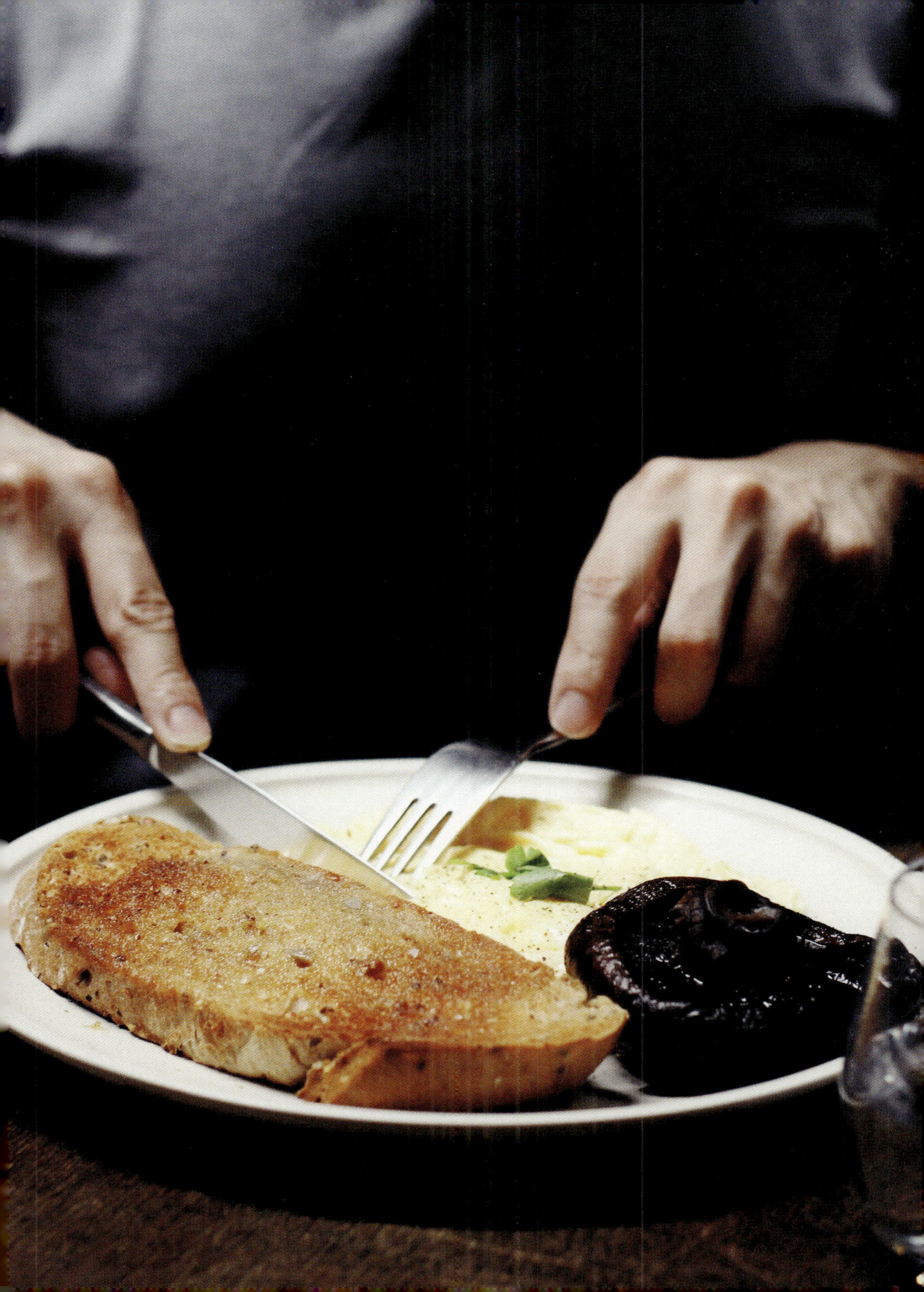

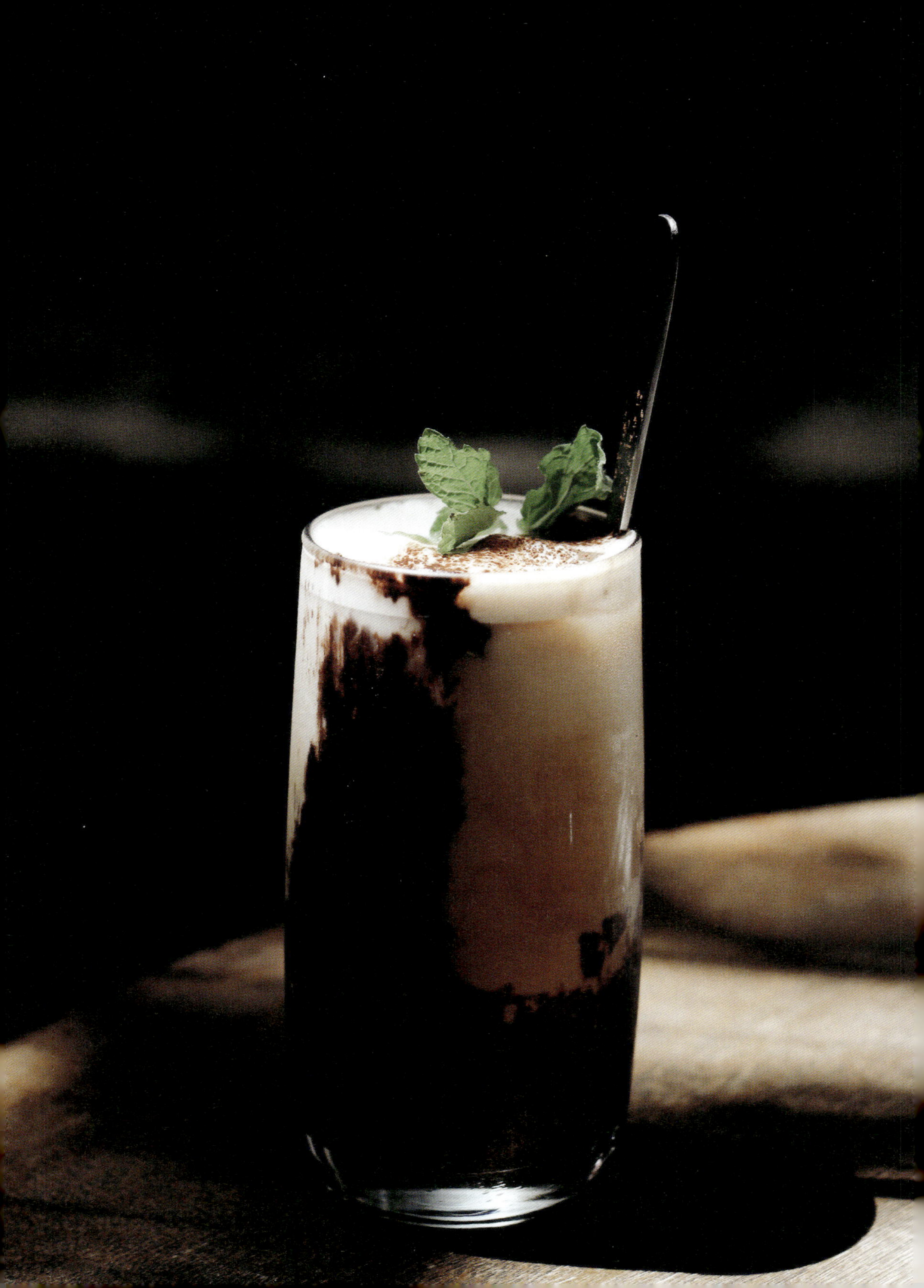

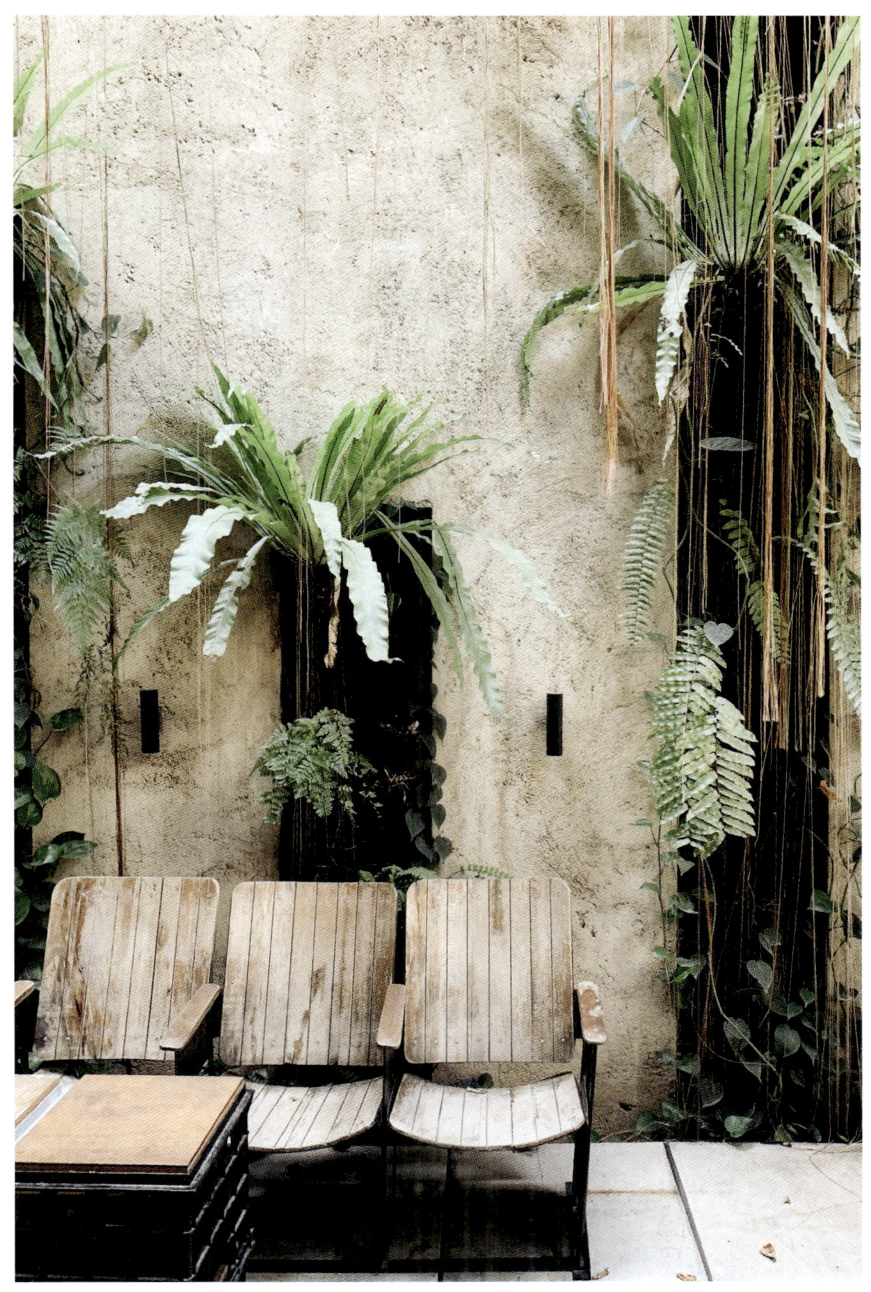

Friday 10:10 AM

Late breakfast at Punch

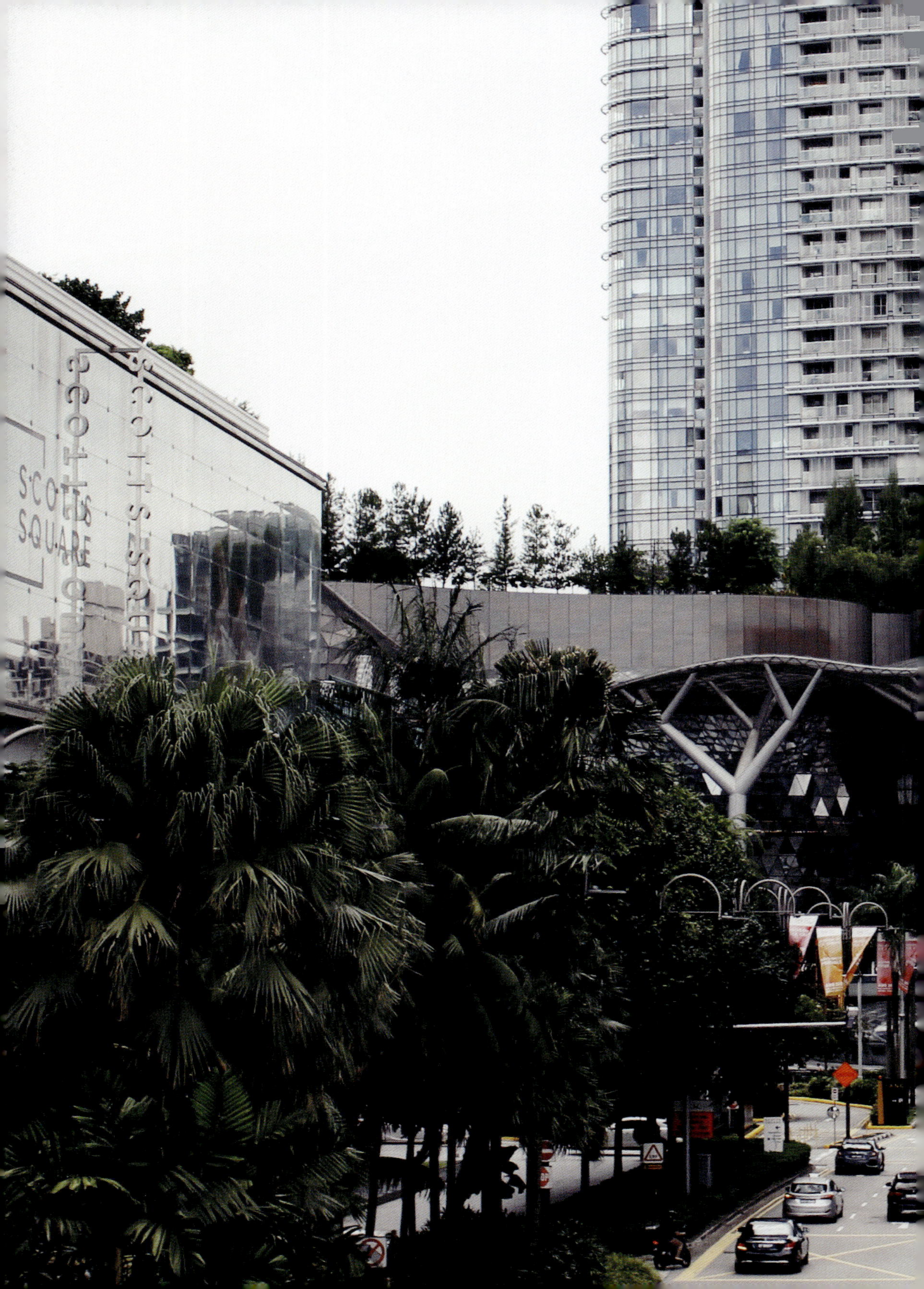

SCOTTS SQUARE

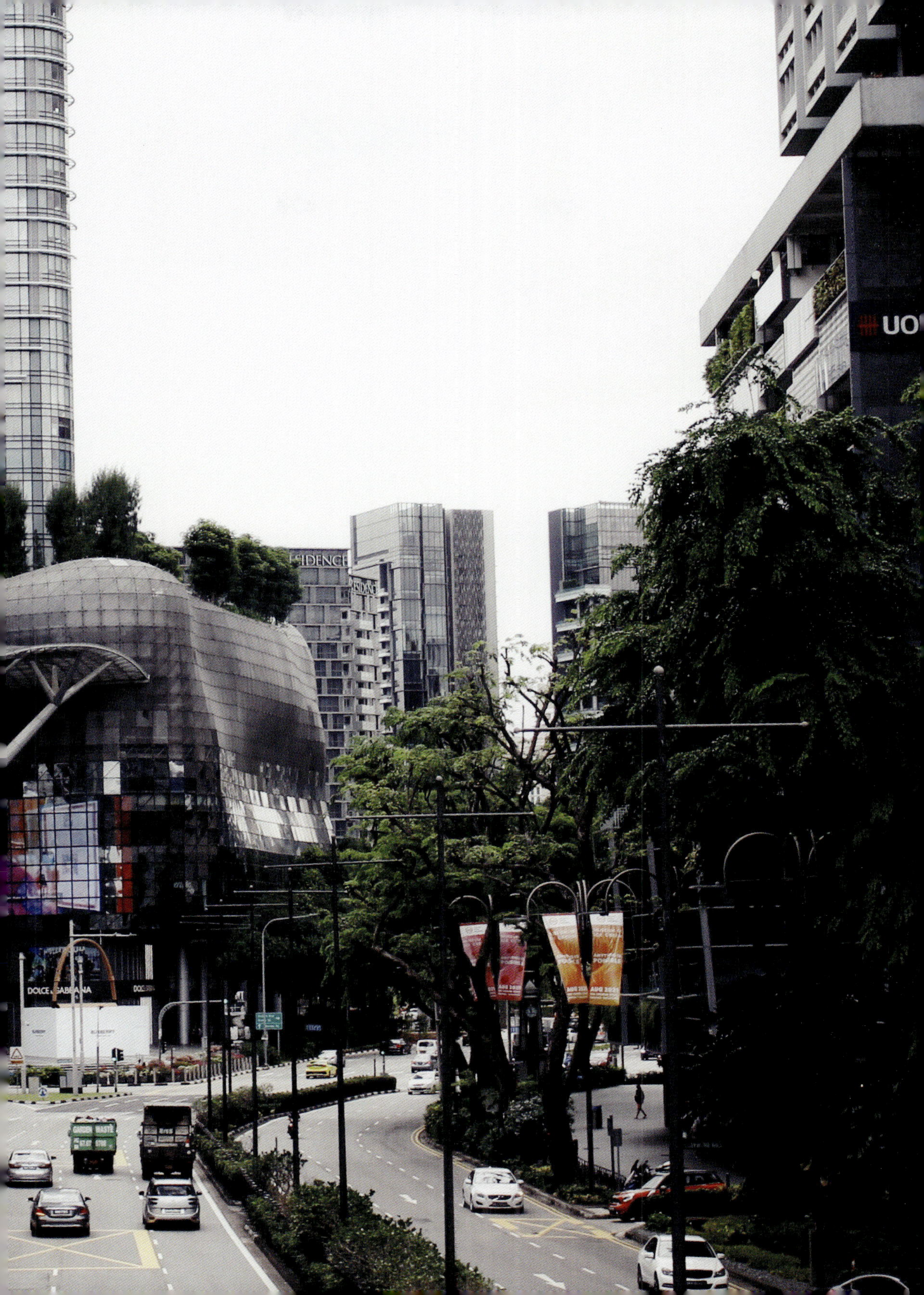

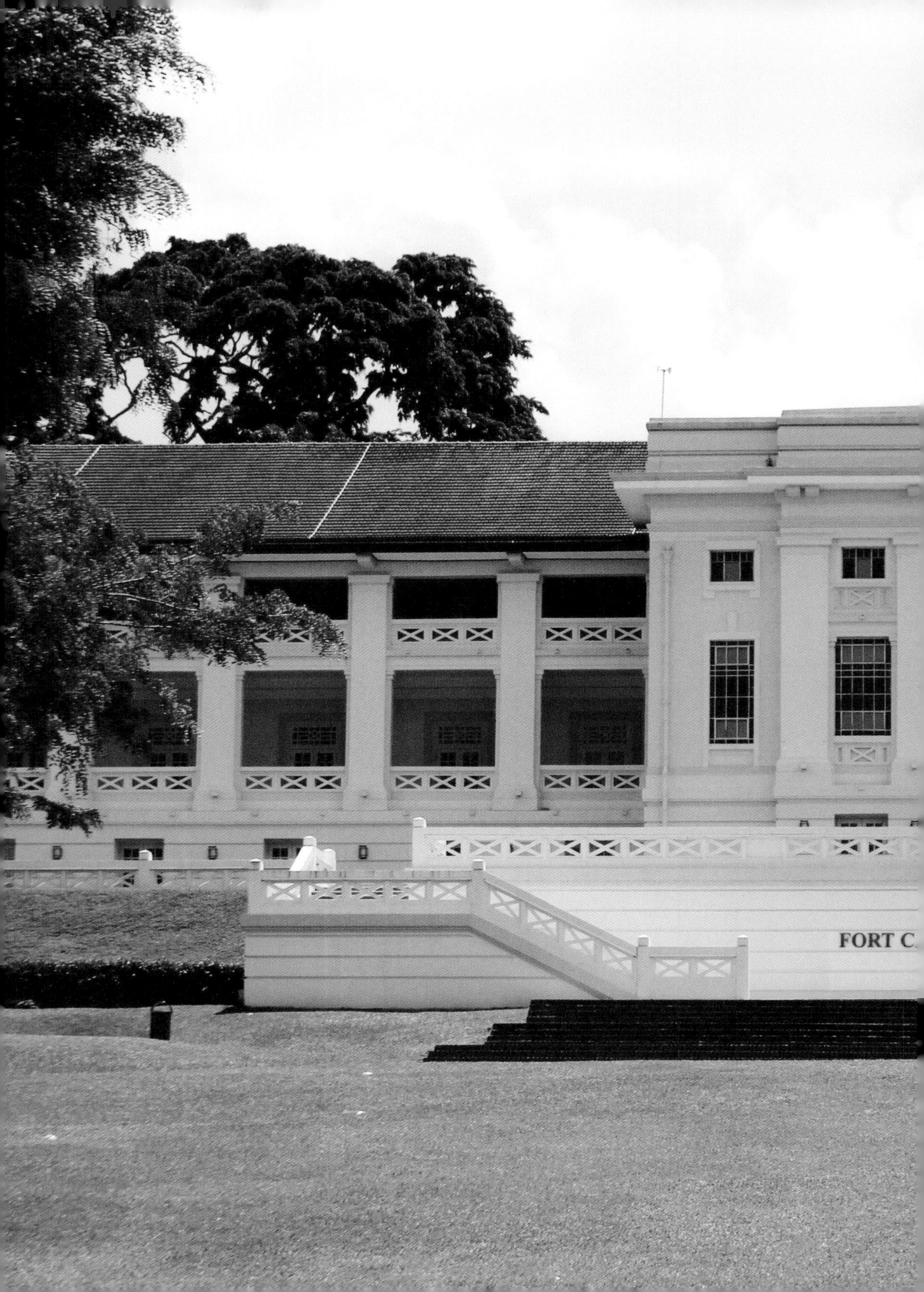

FORT C

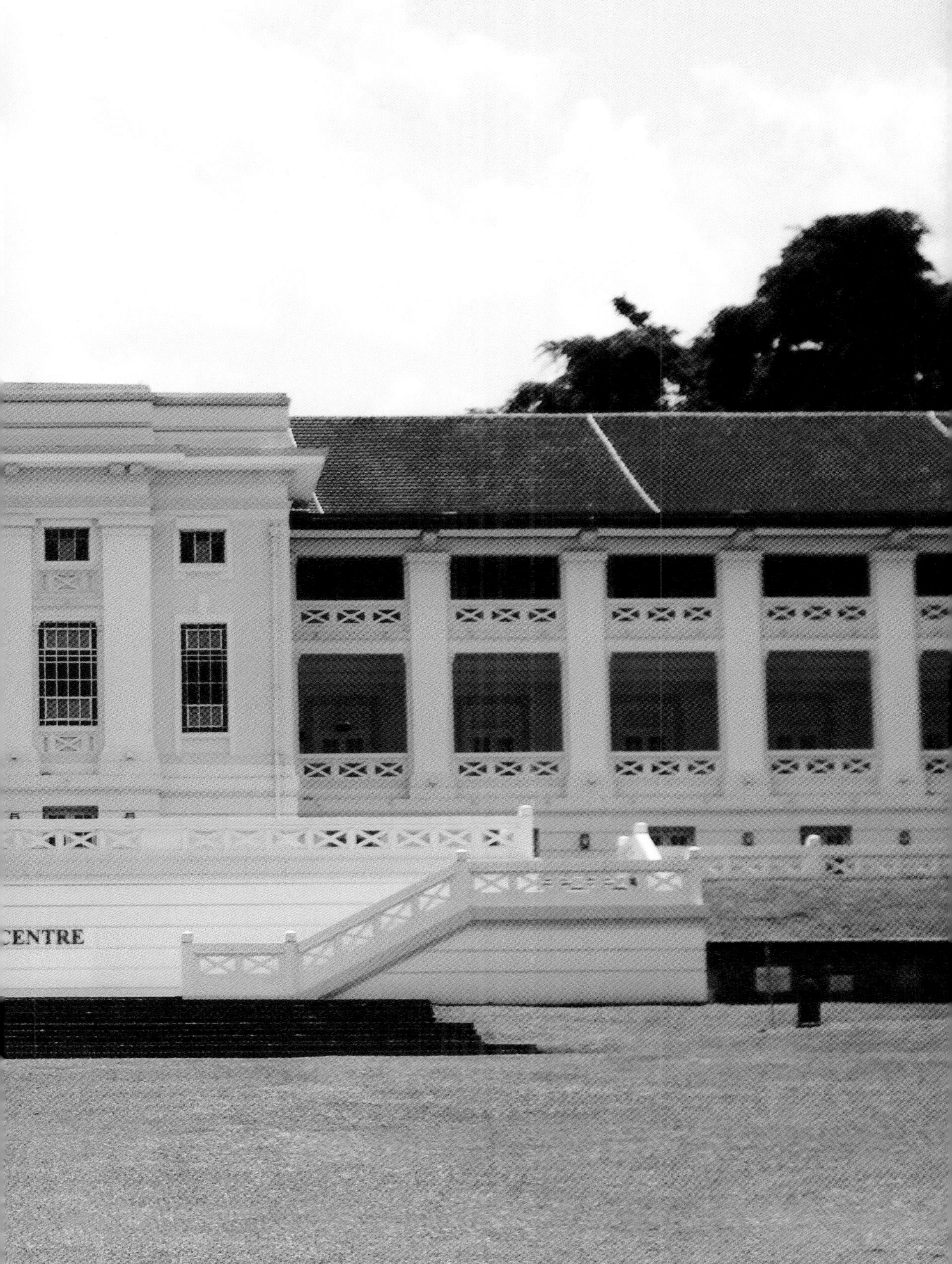
CENTRE

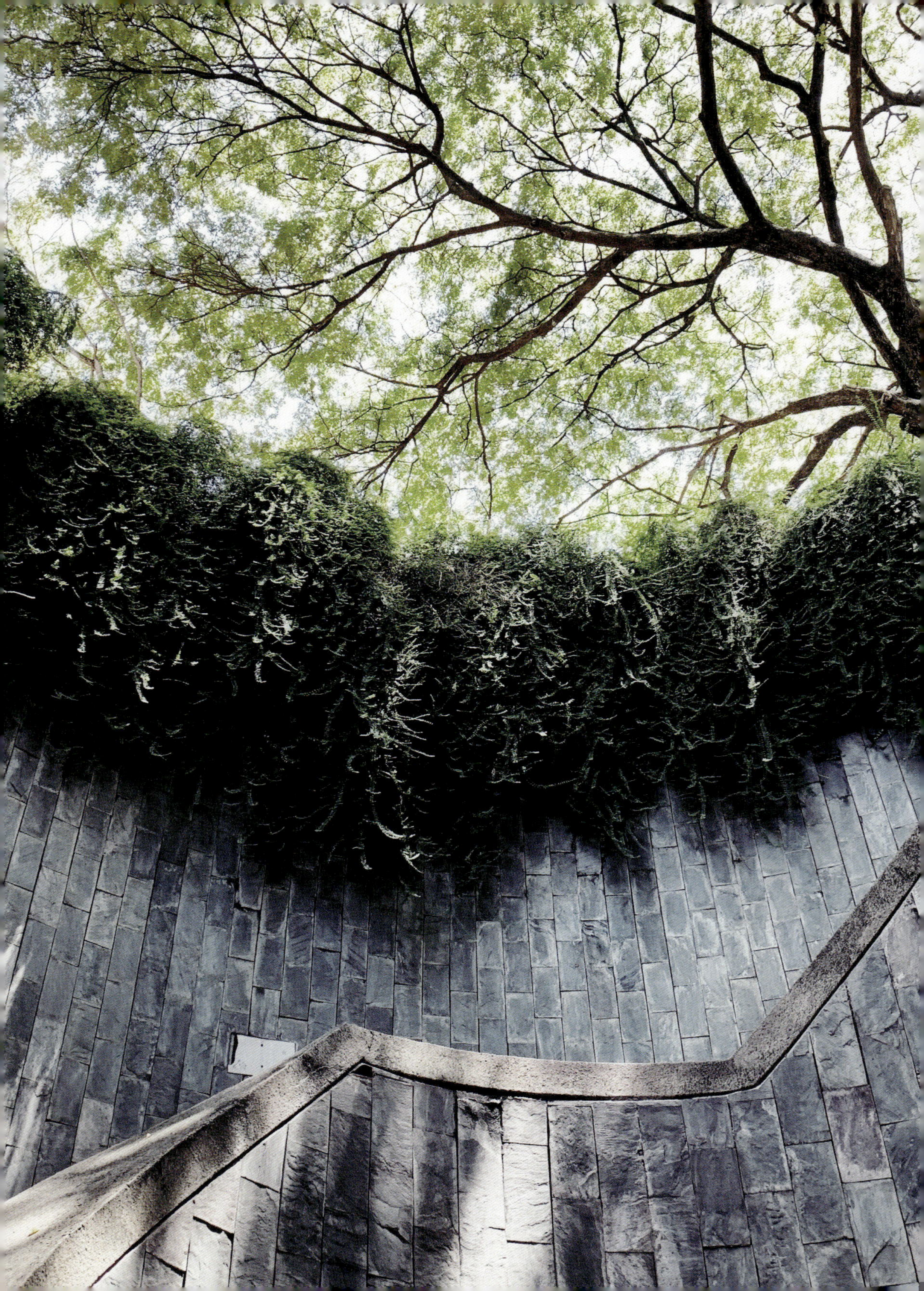

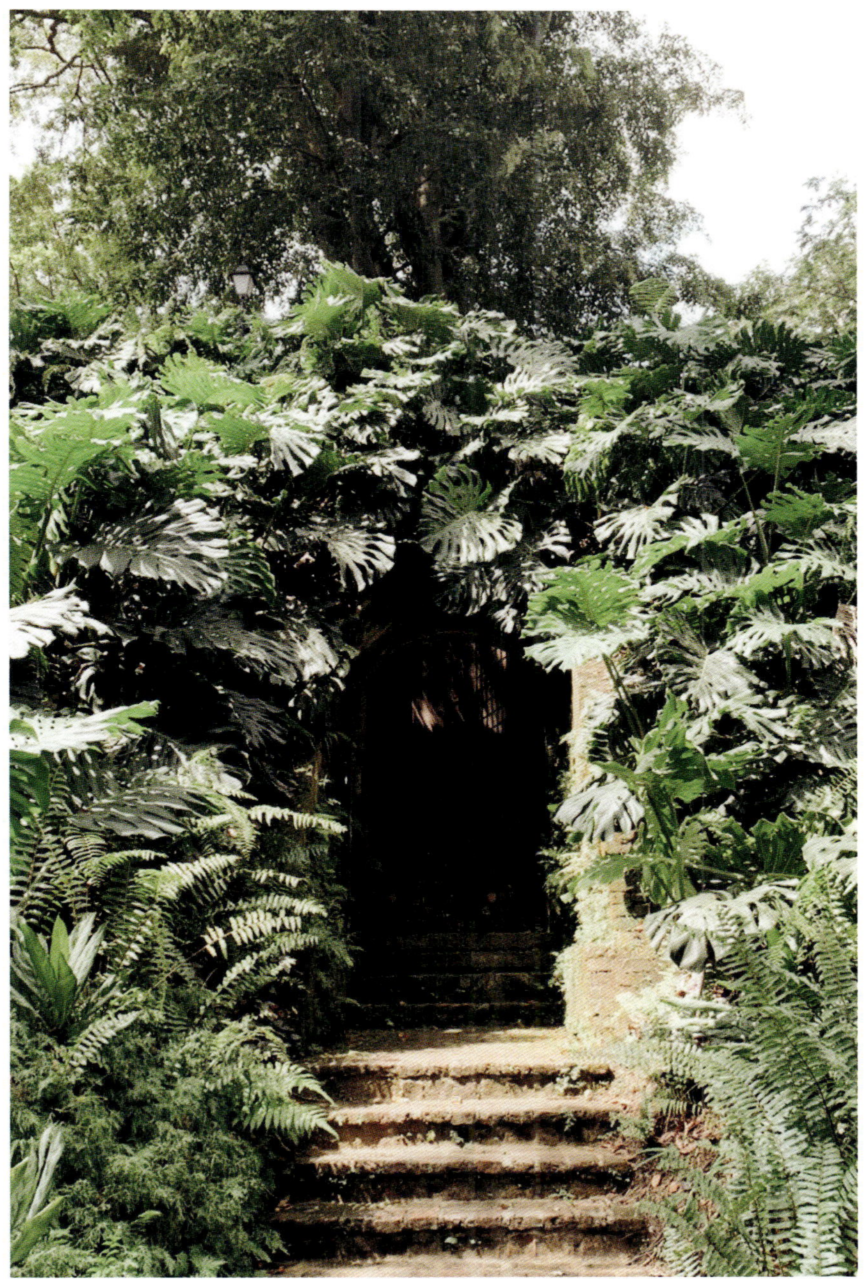



Exploring Fort Canning

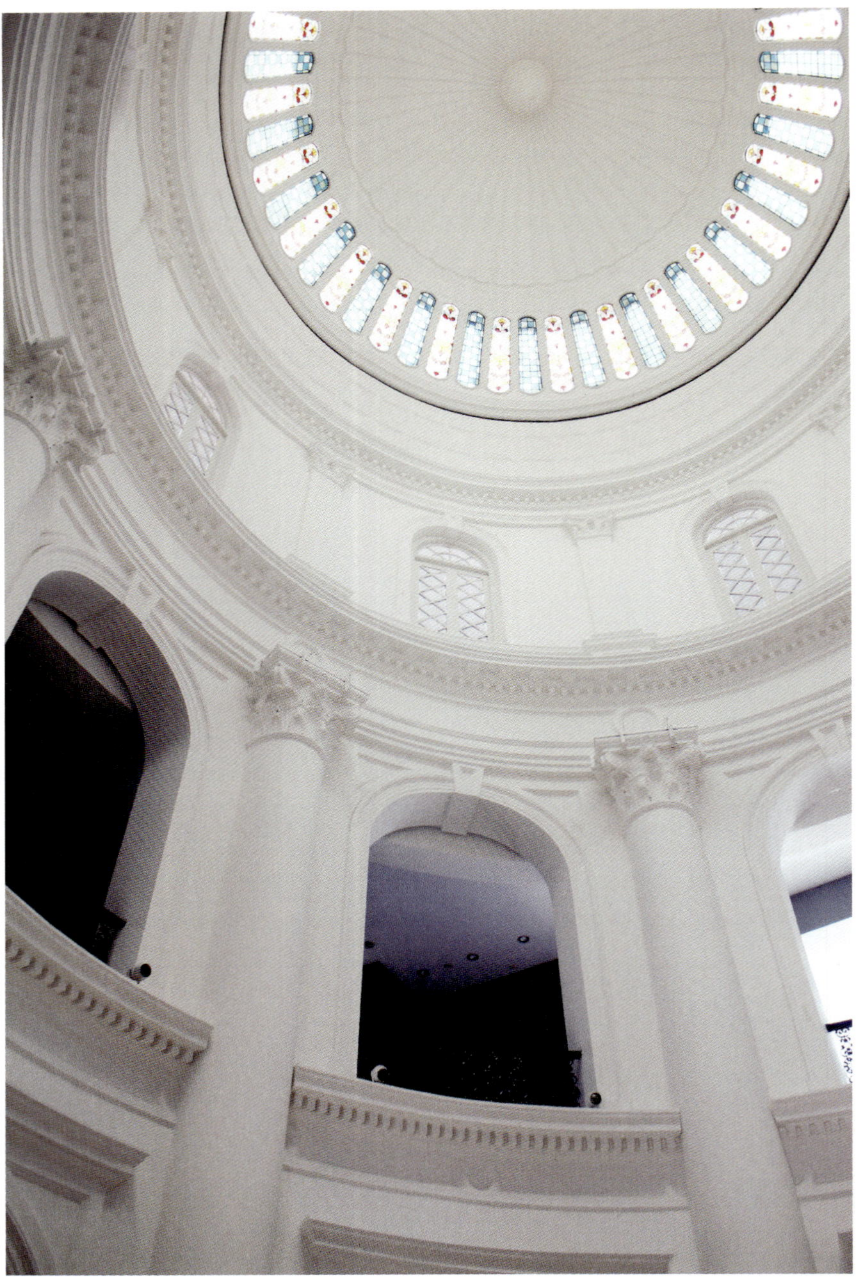

National Museum                    Friday 1:20 PM

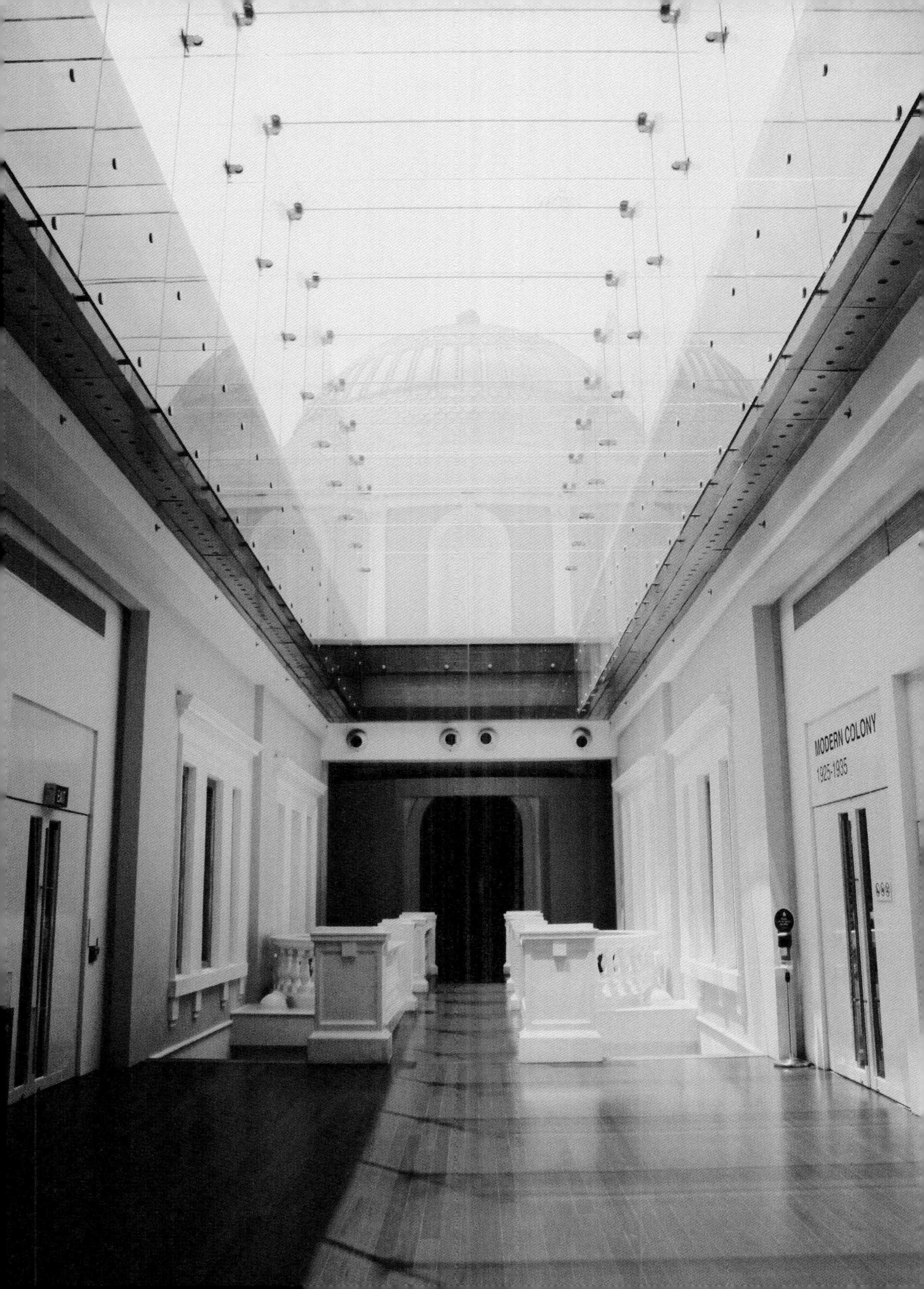

EXIT
MODERN COLONY
1925-1935

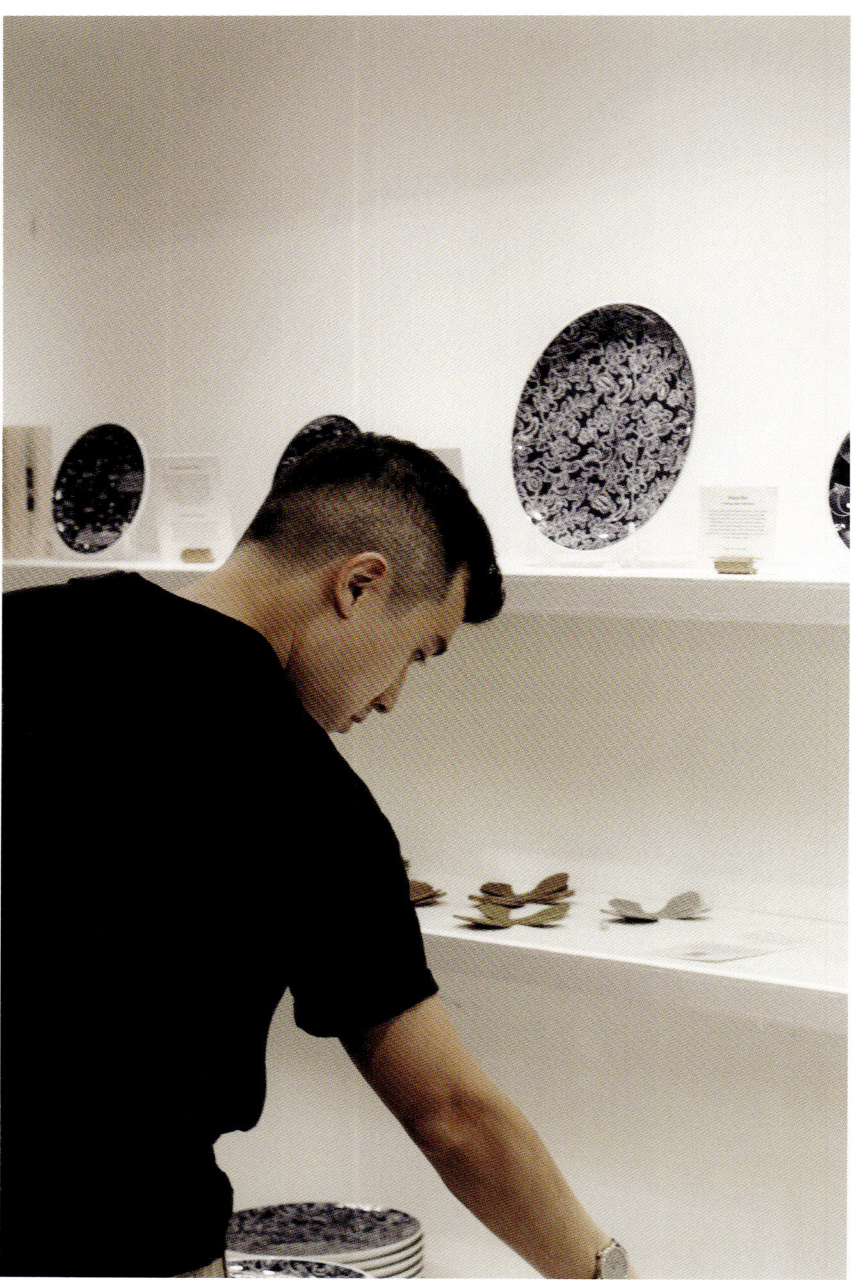

Supermama Store                                    Friday 2:10 PM

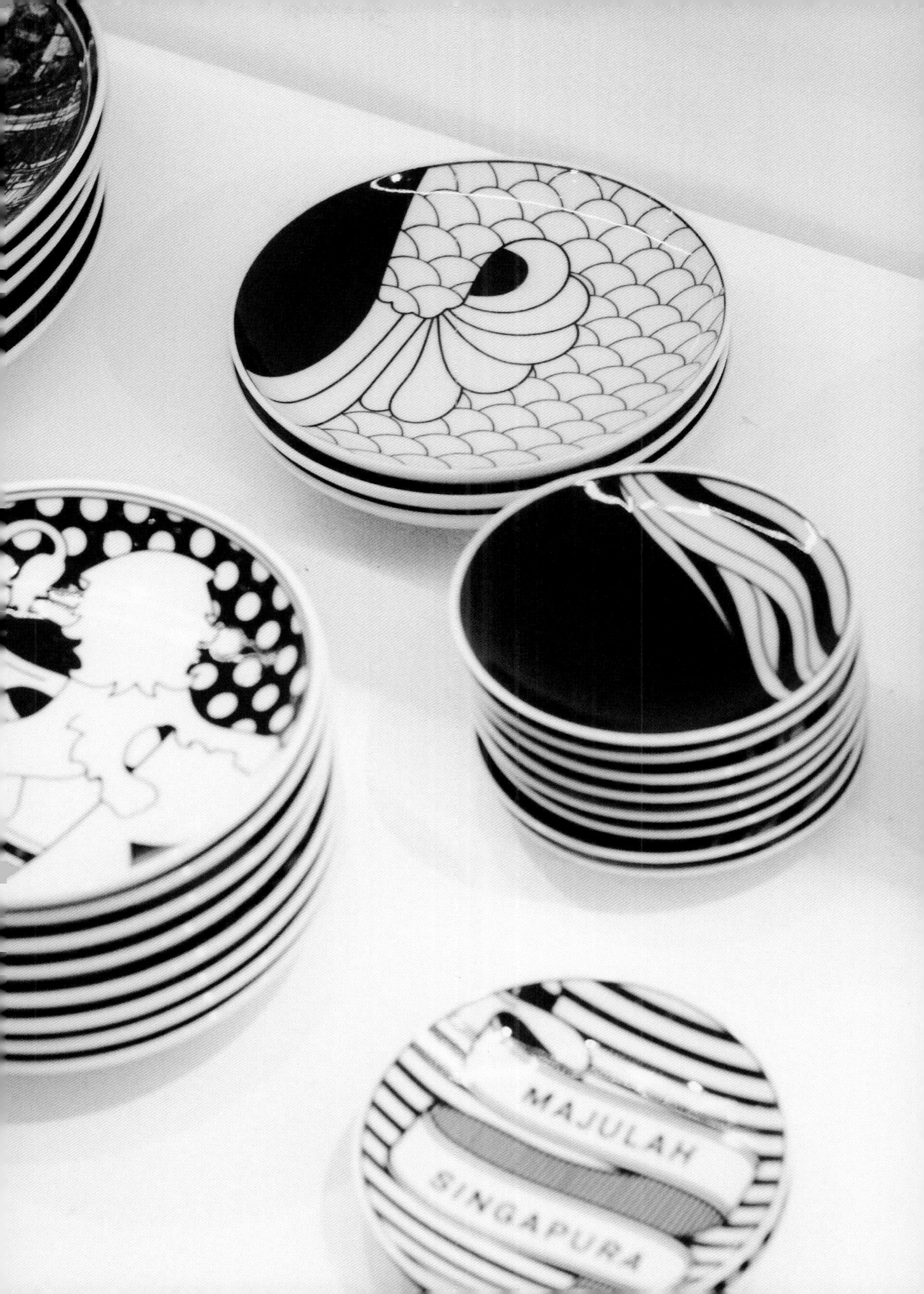
MAJULAH
SINGAPURA

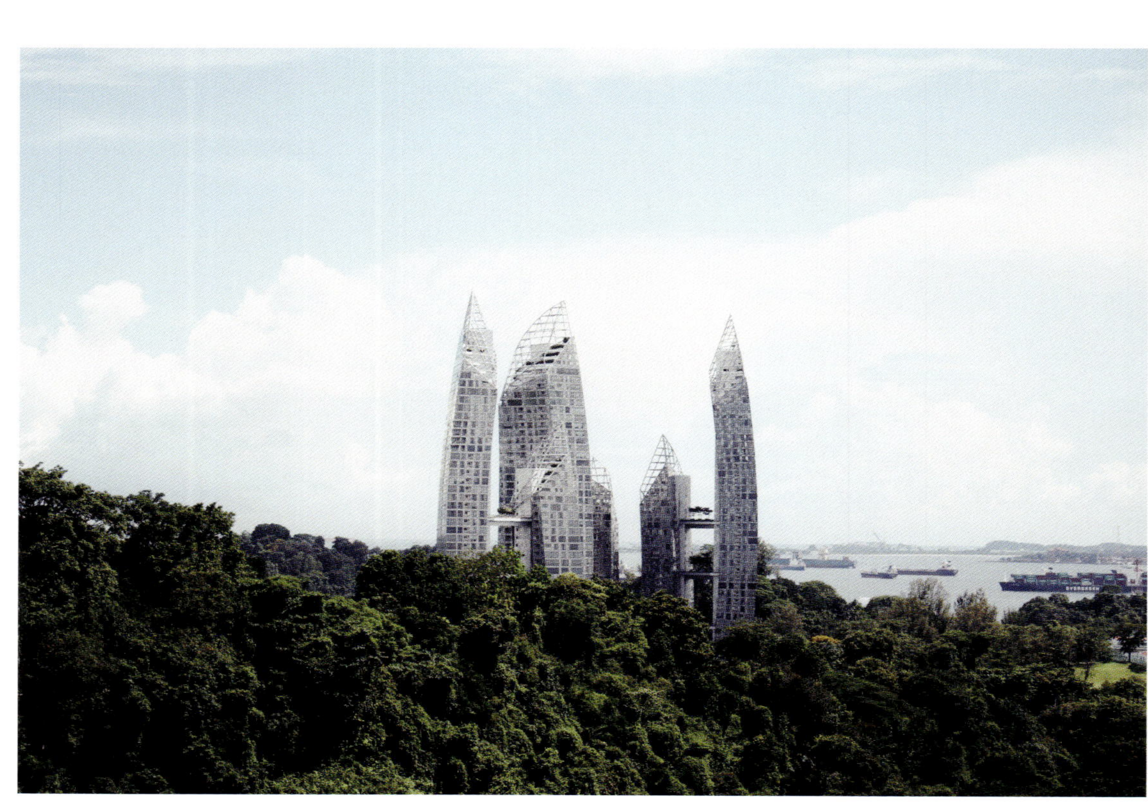

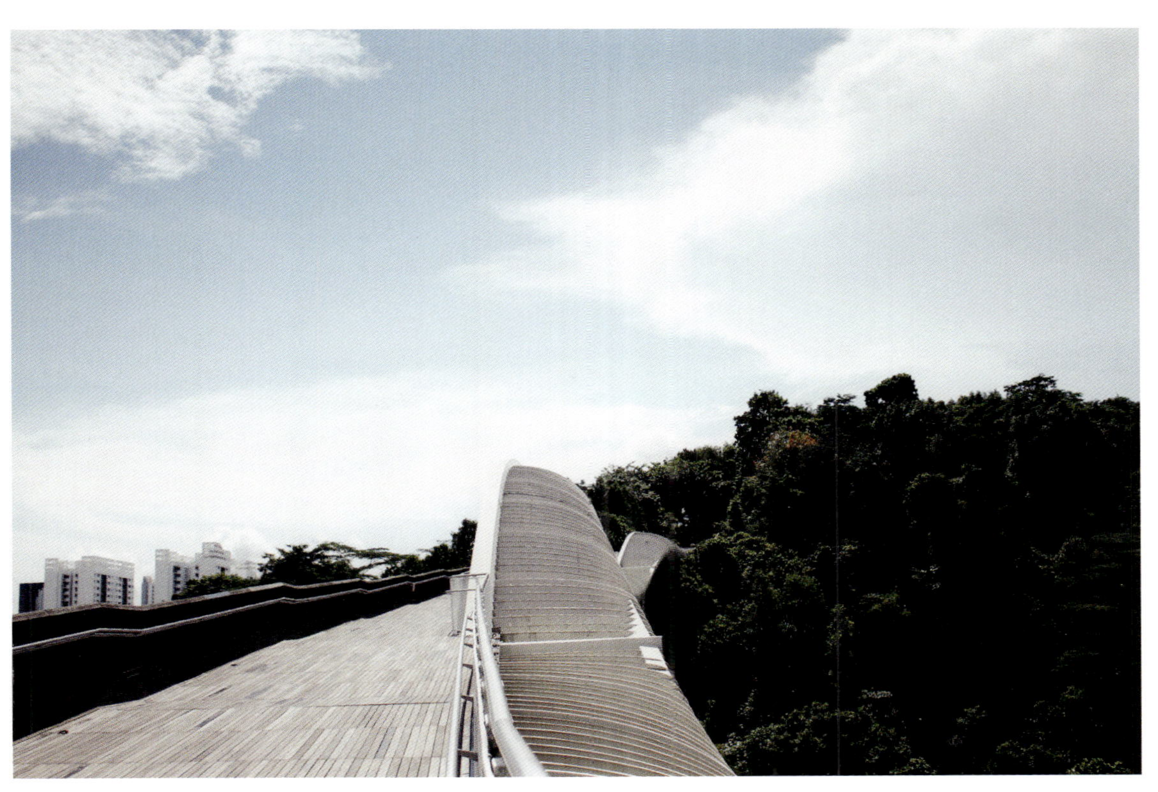

Friday 3:05 PM                                          Henderson Waves

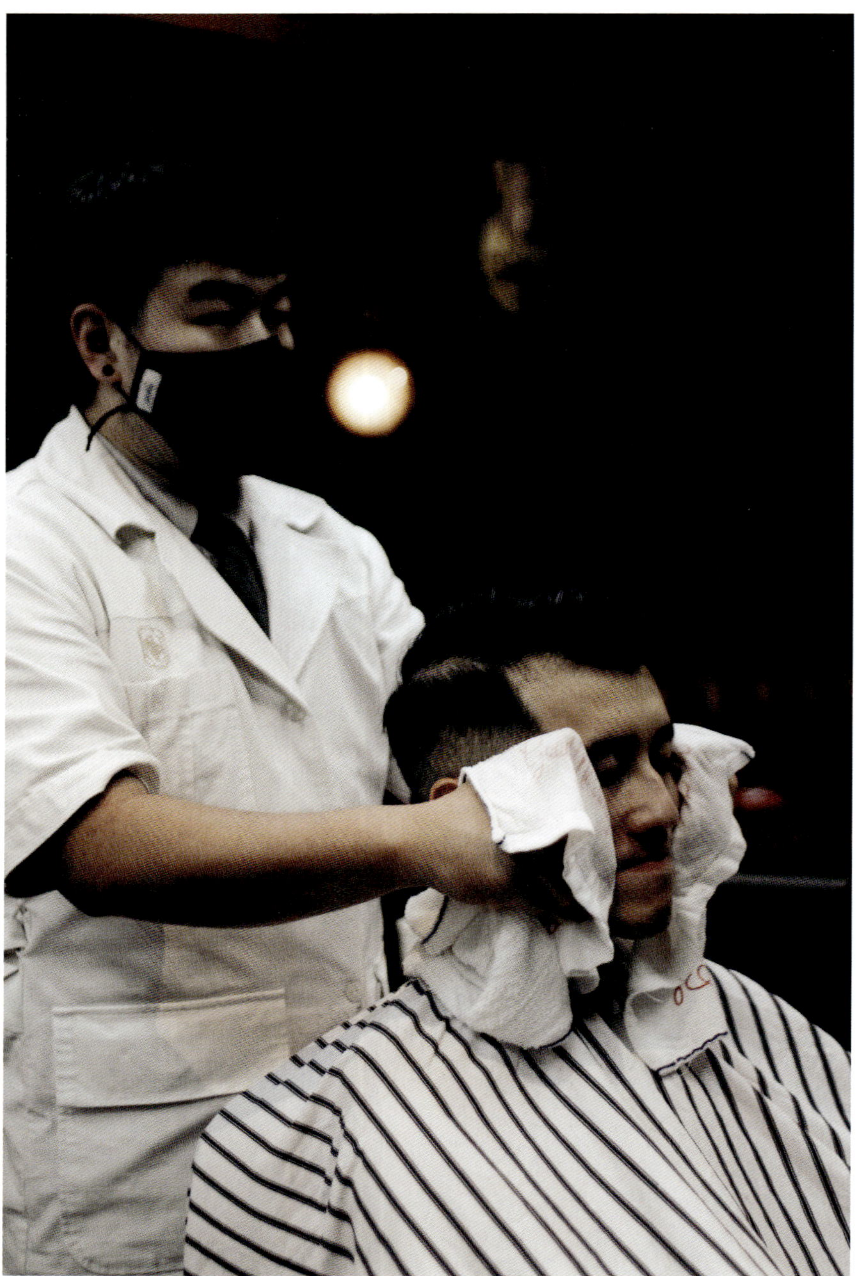



Haircut at Hounds of the Baskervilles                                    Friday 4:30 PM

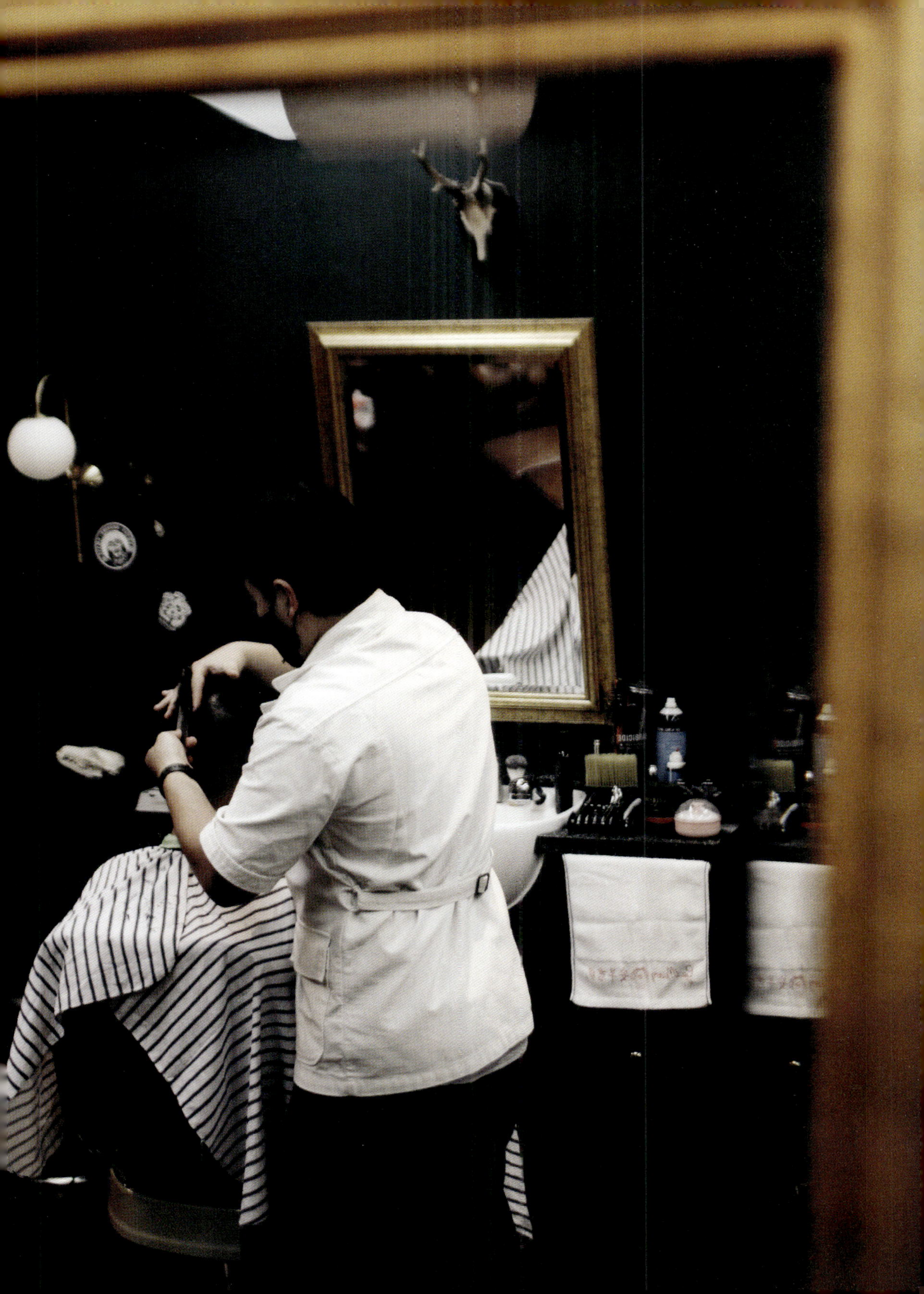

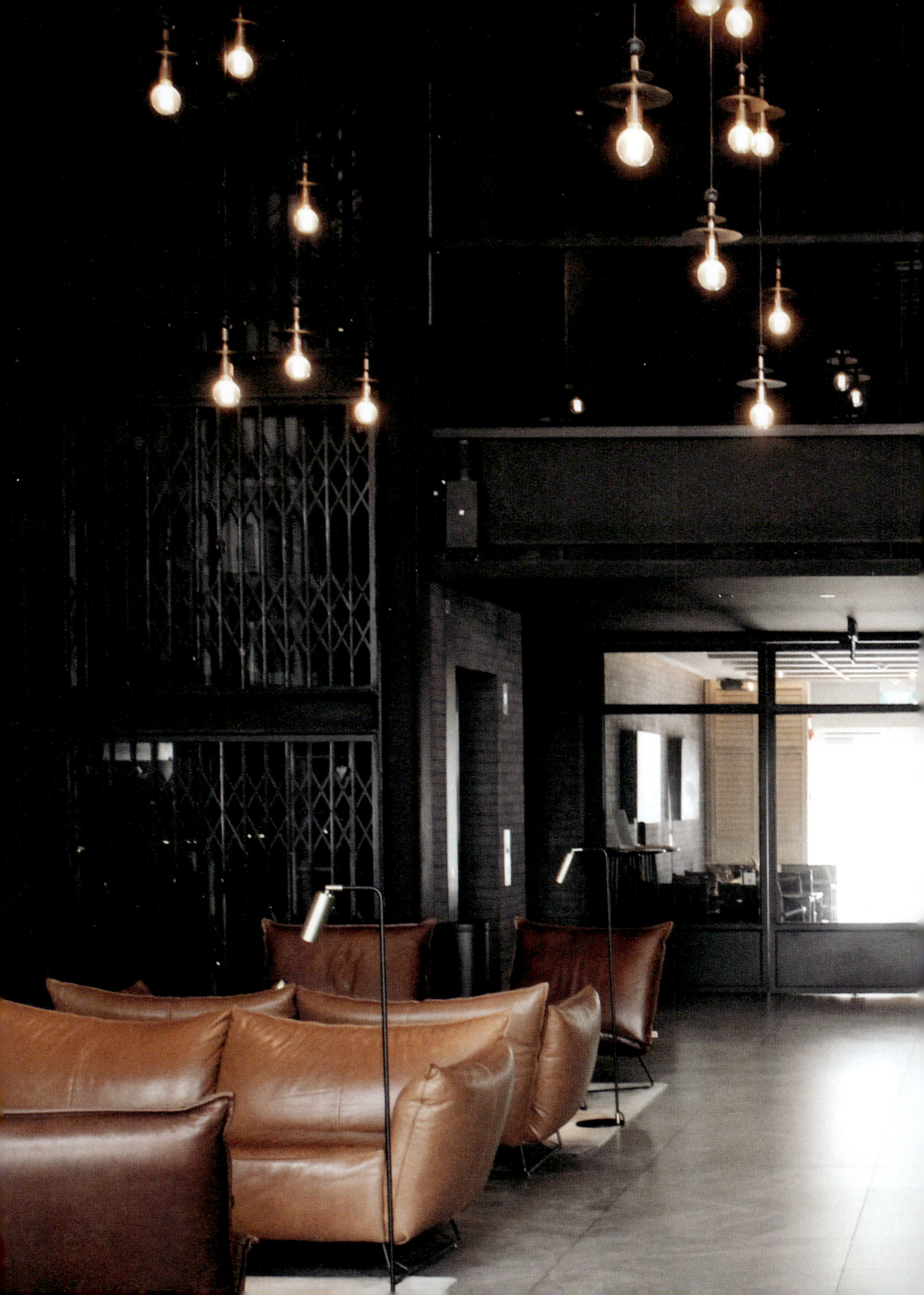

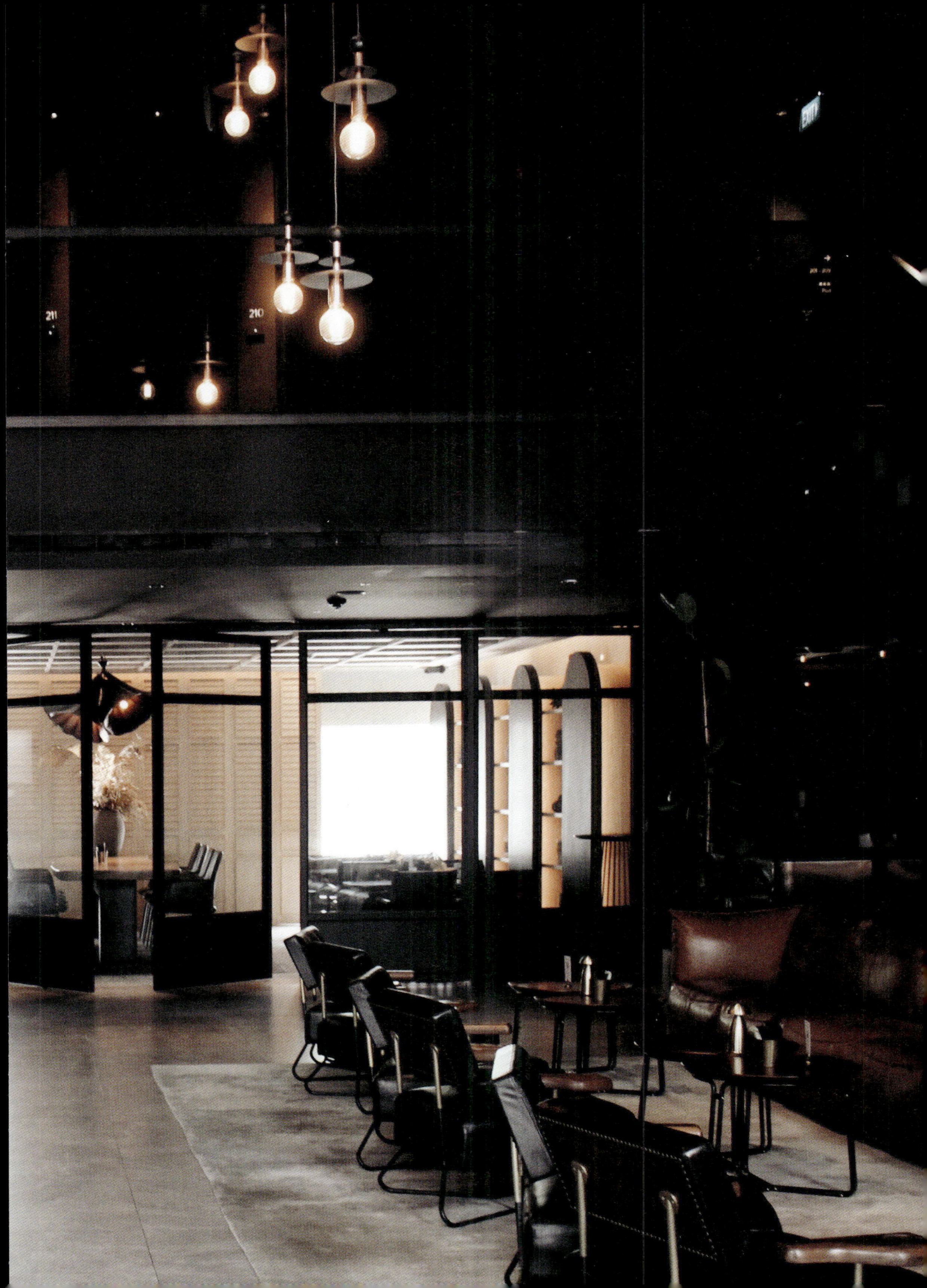

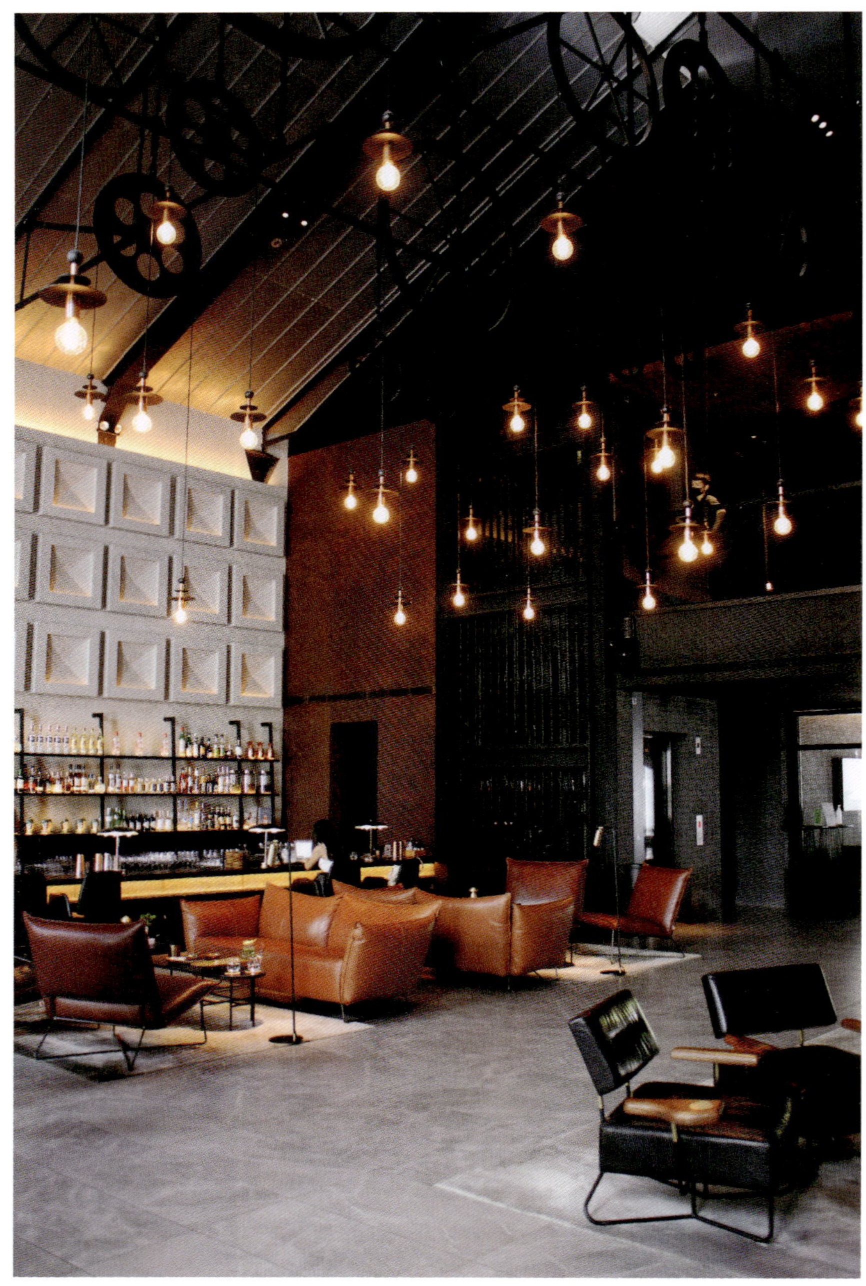

An evening tipple at the Lobby Bar                    Friday 6:15 PM

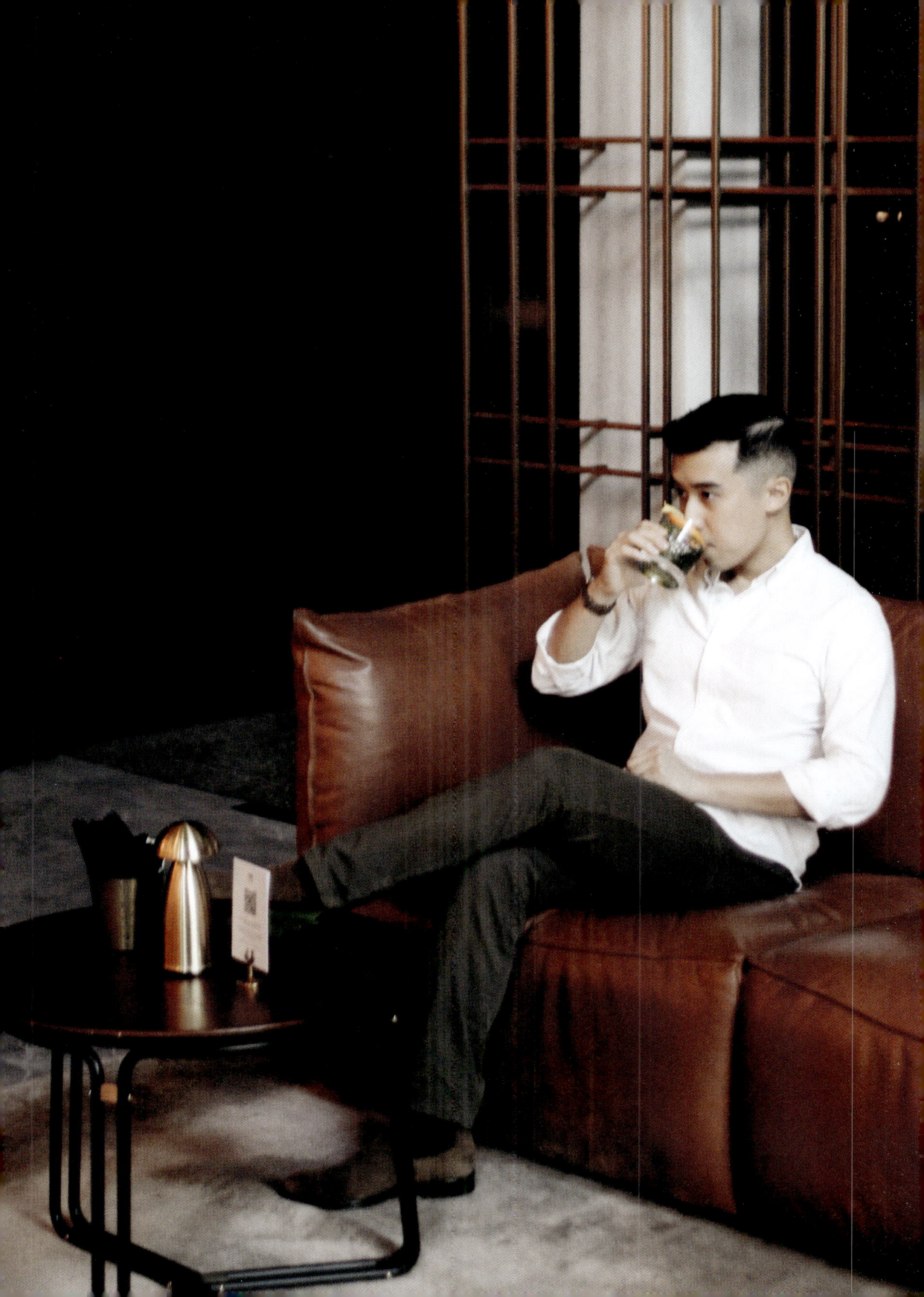

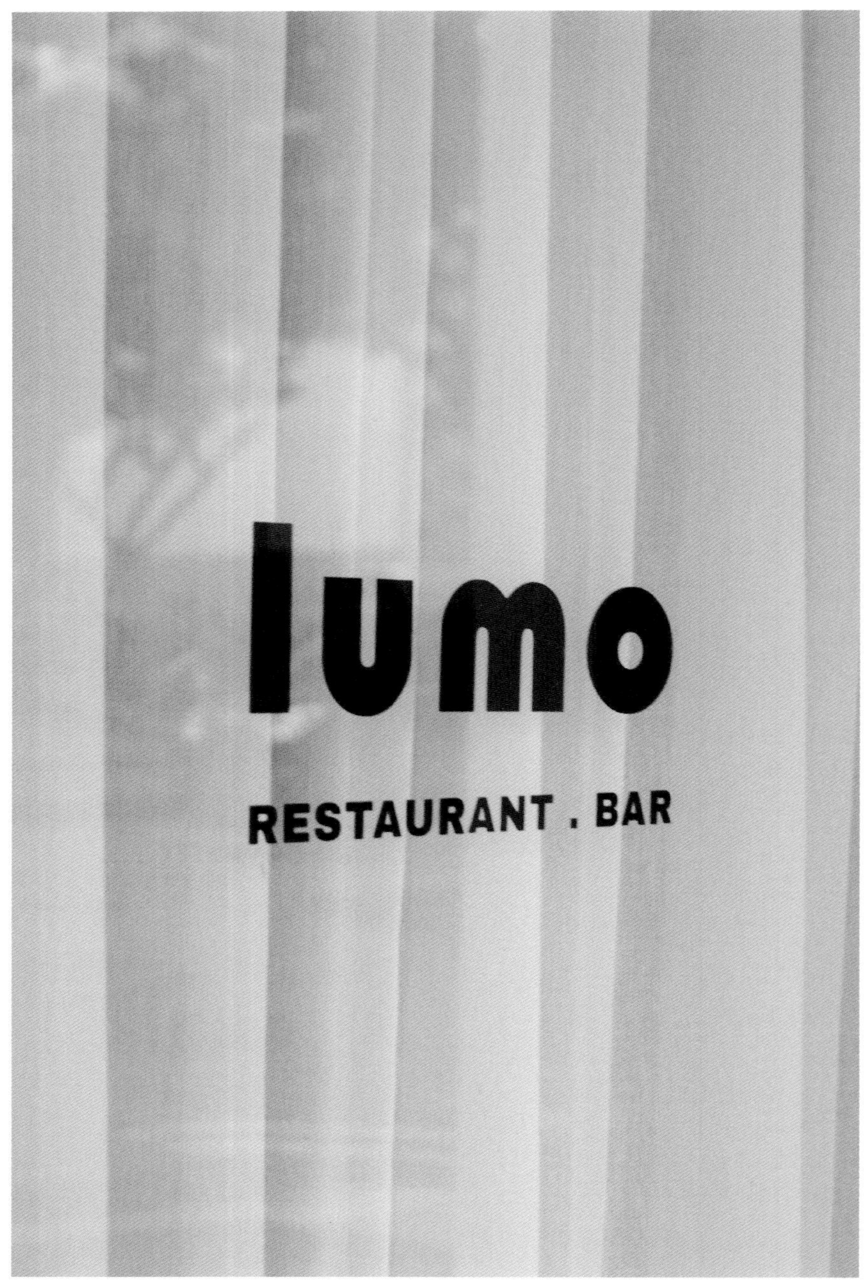


Dinner at Lumo                    Friday 7:20 PM

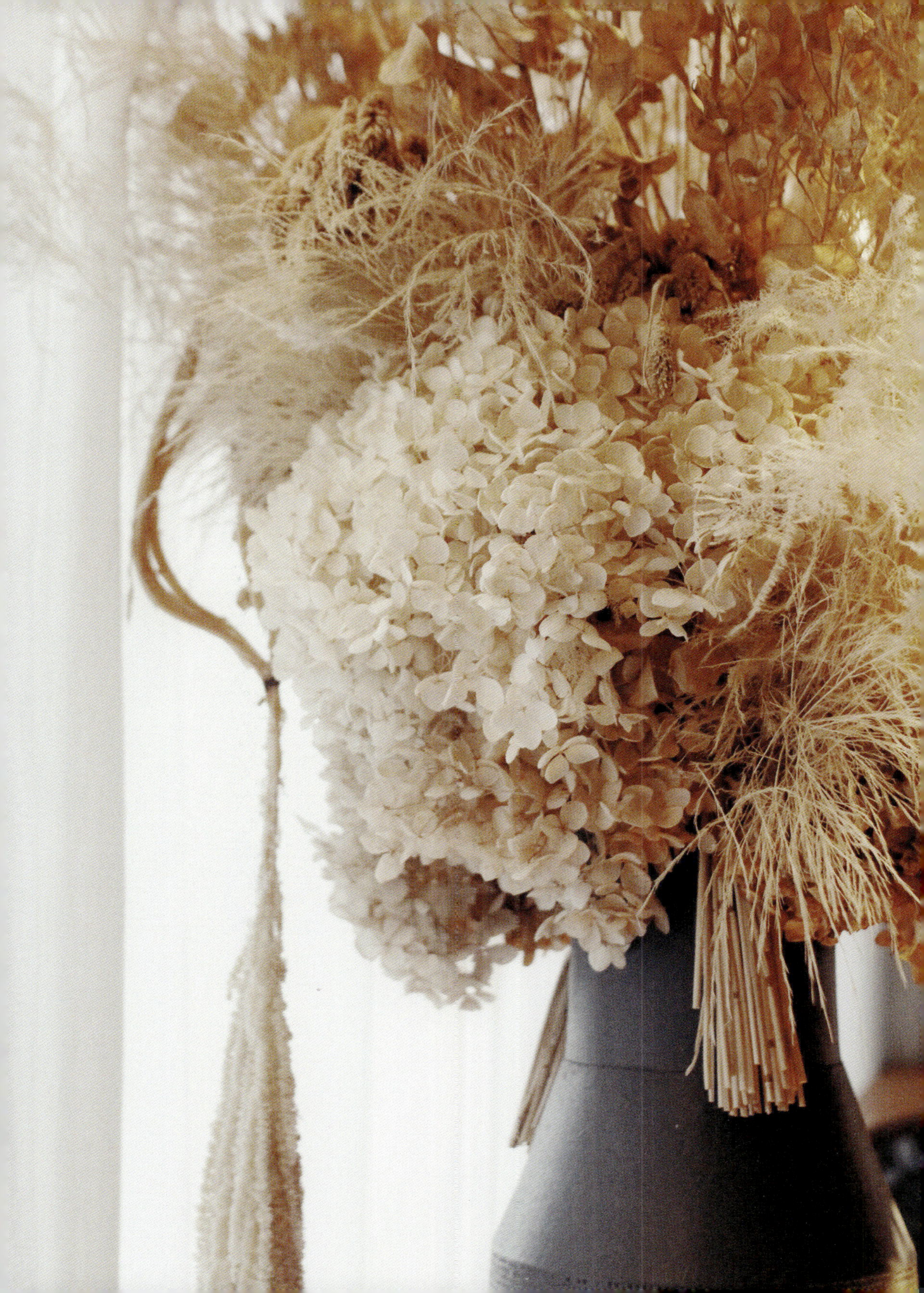

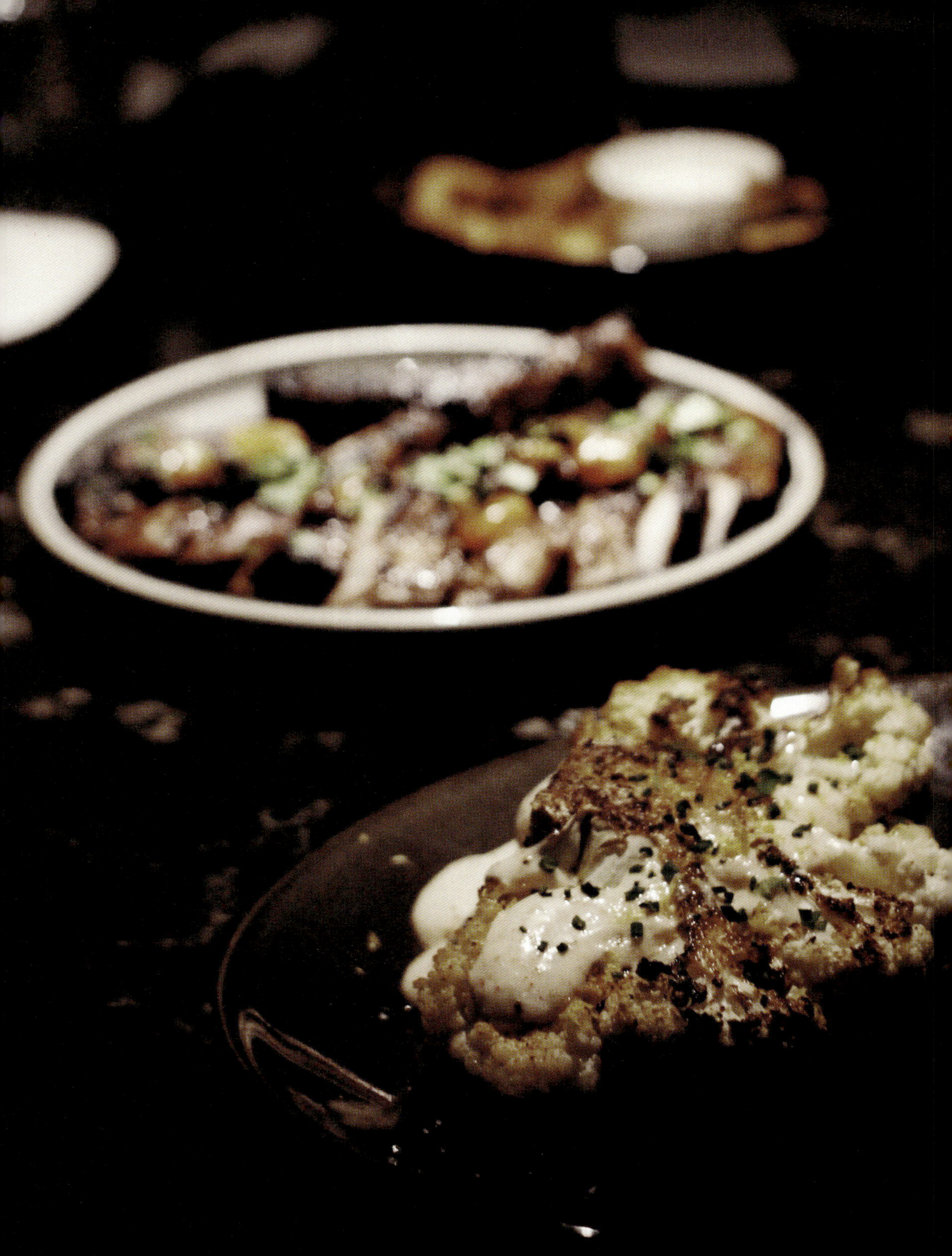

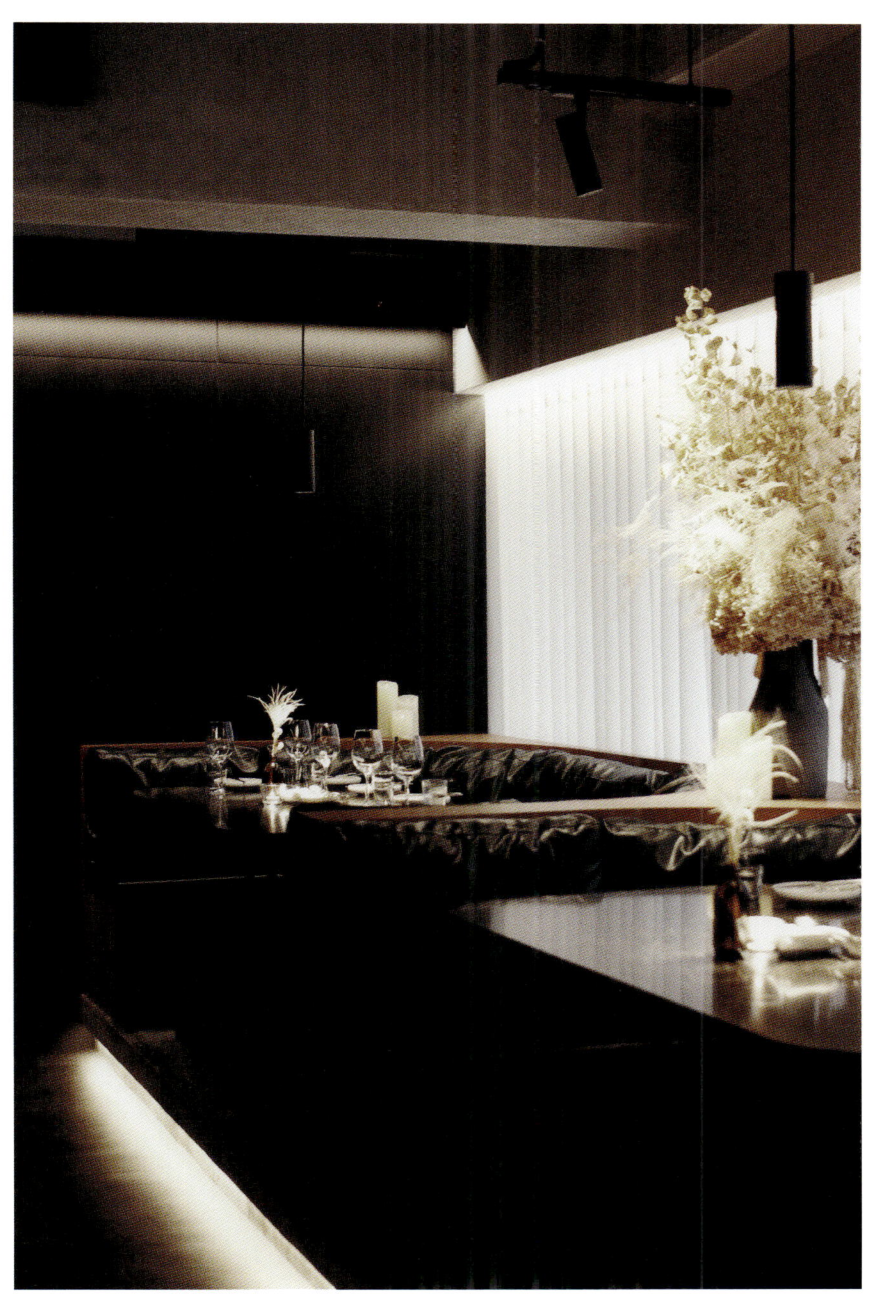

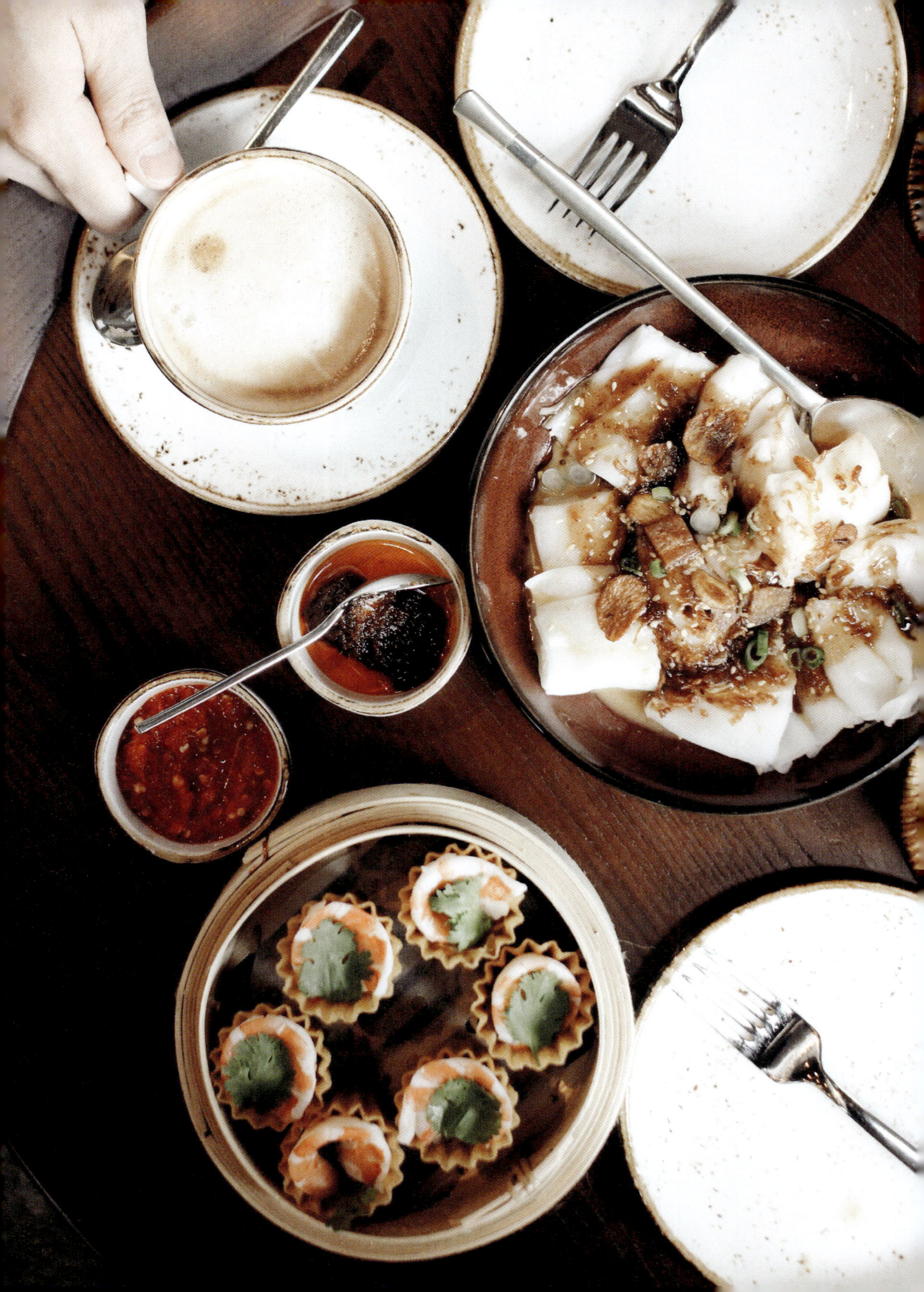

# Saturday

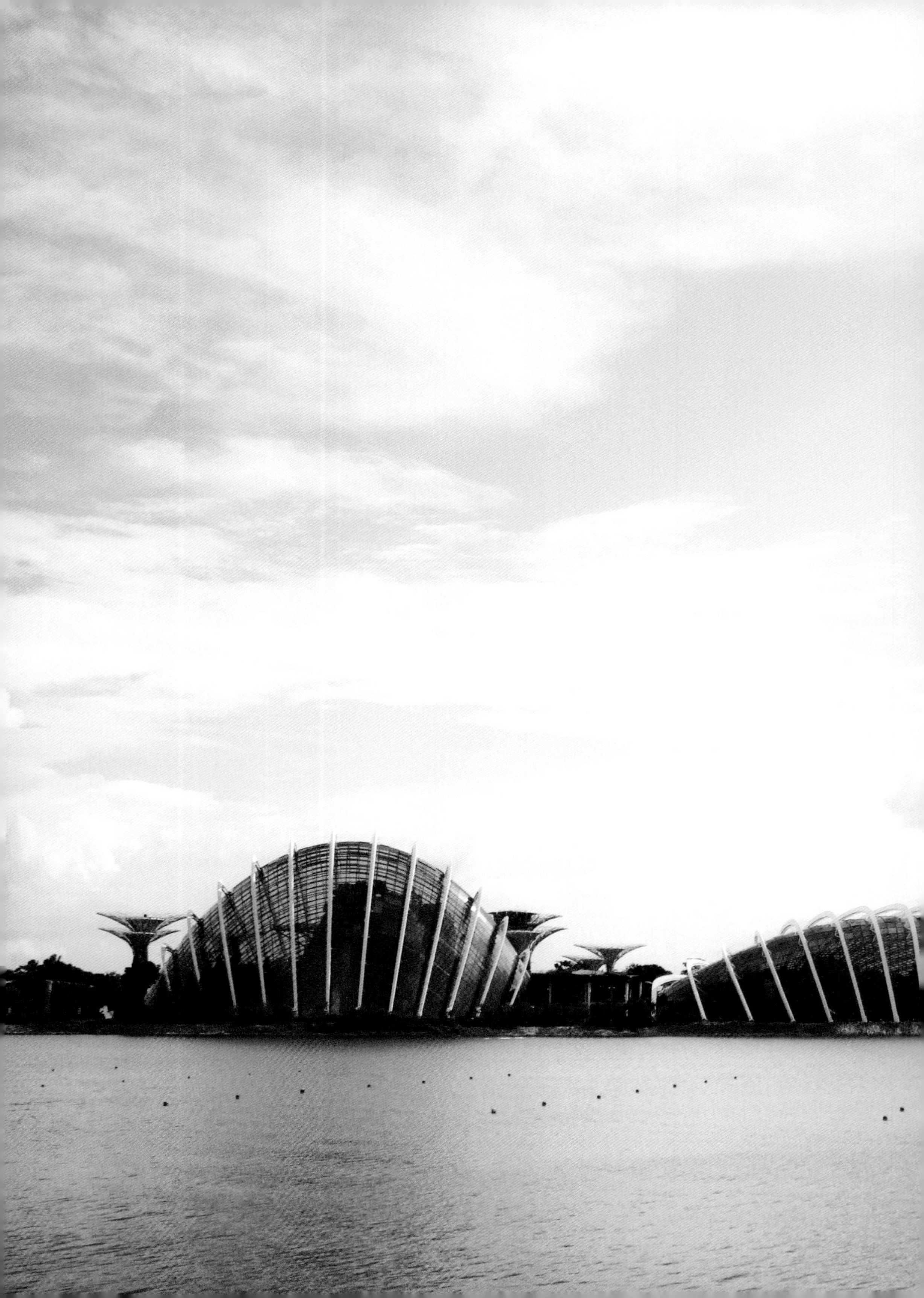

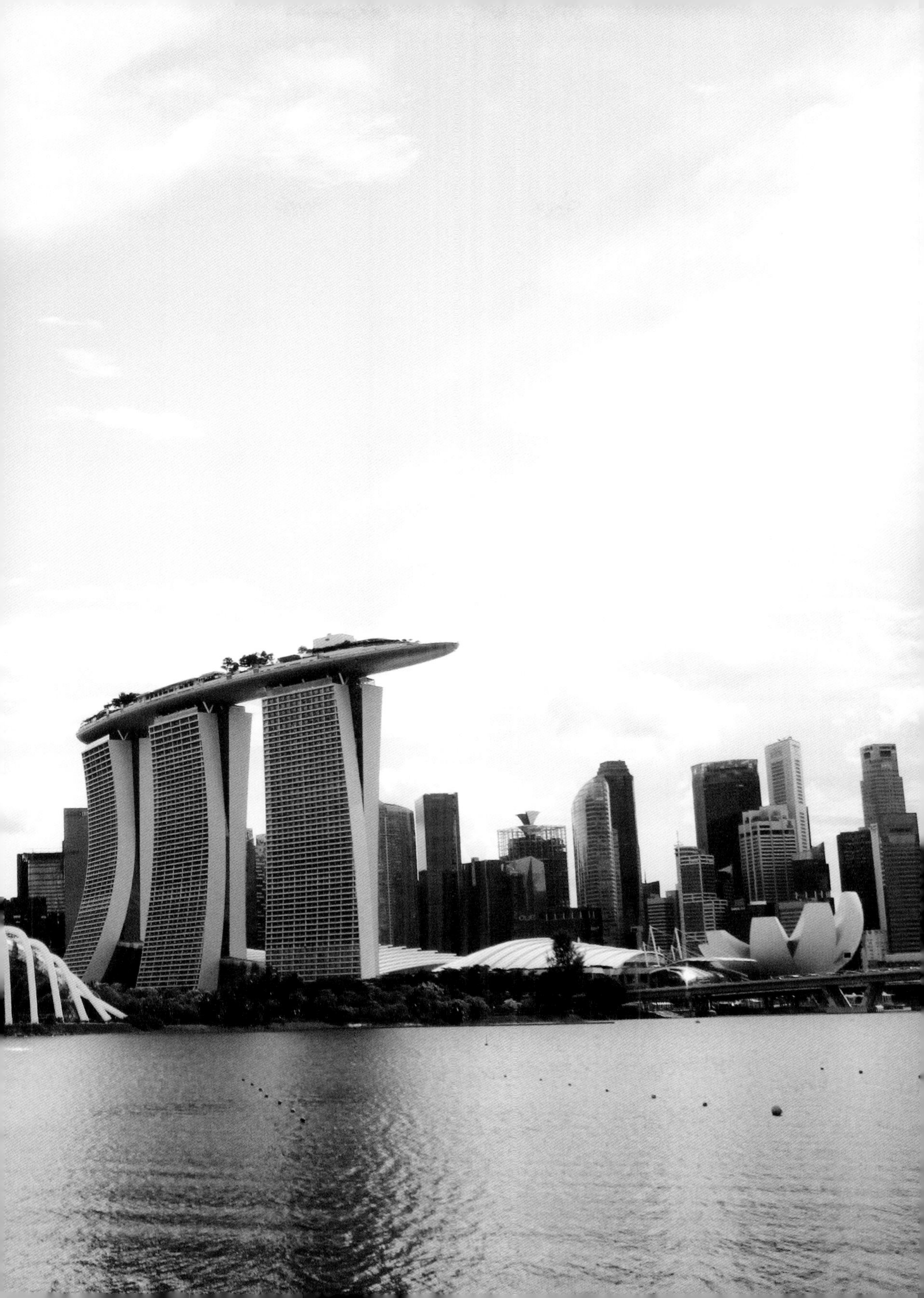

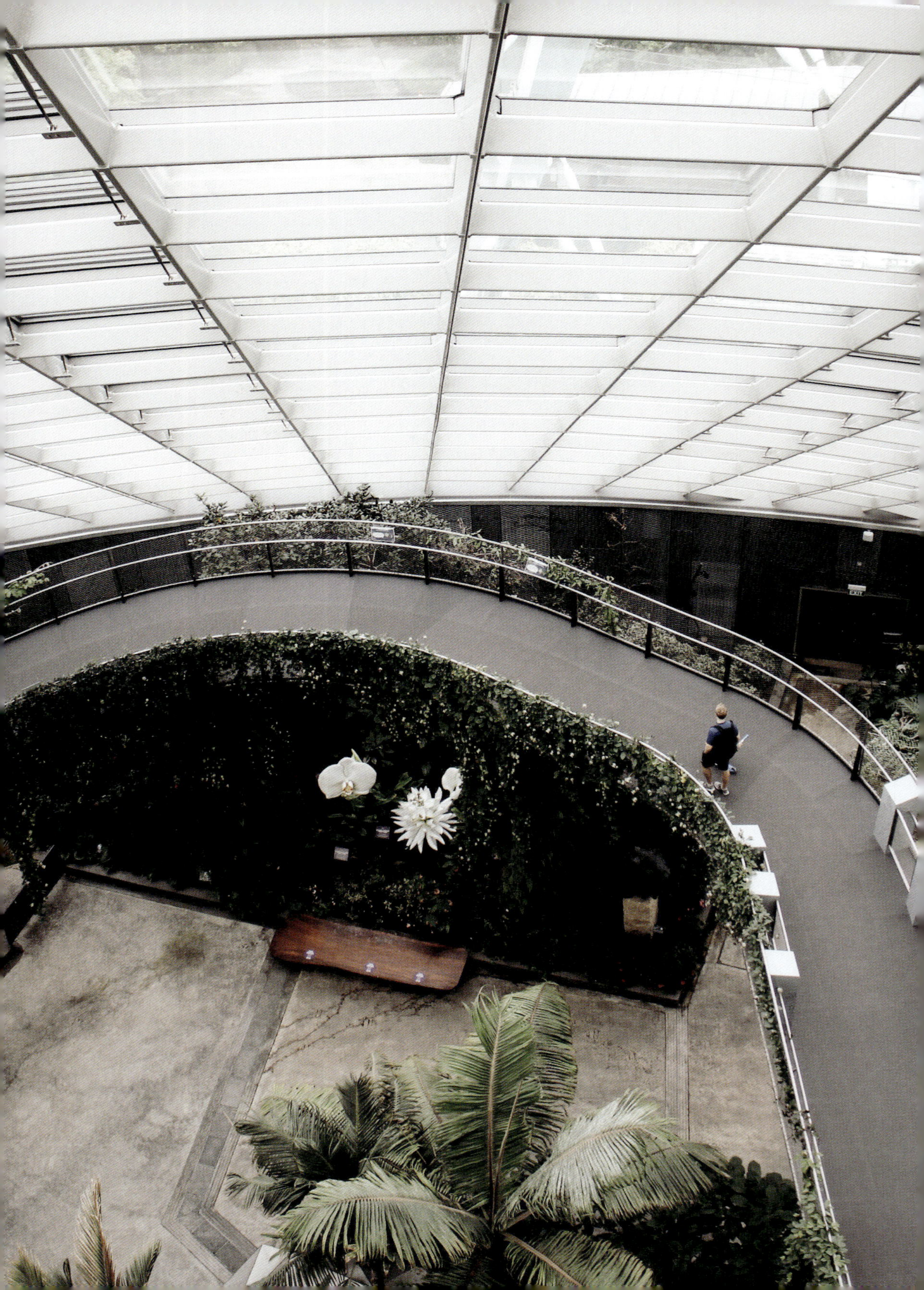

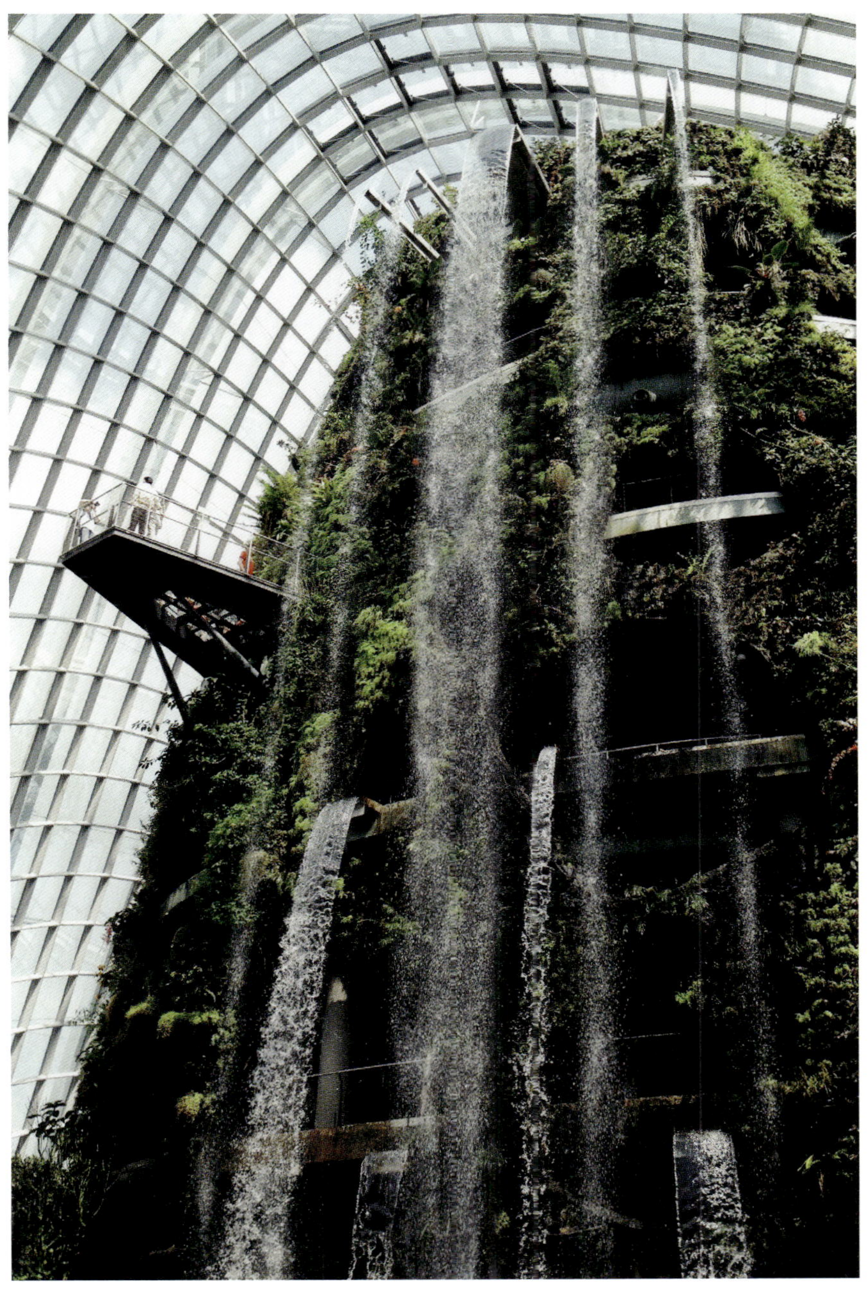



Gardens by the Bay

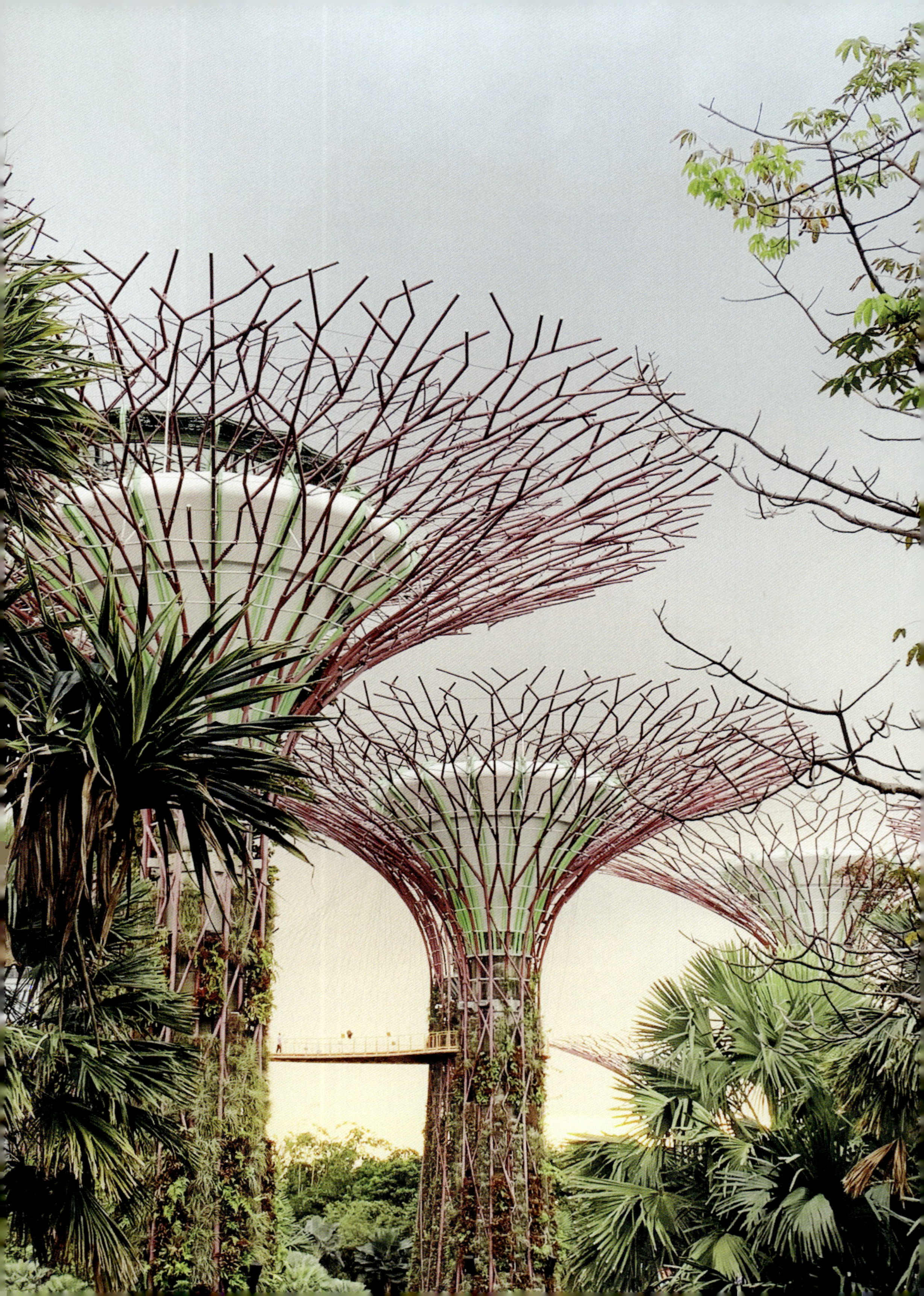

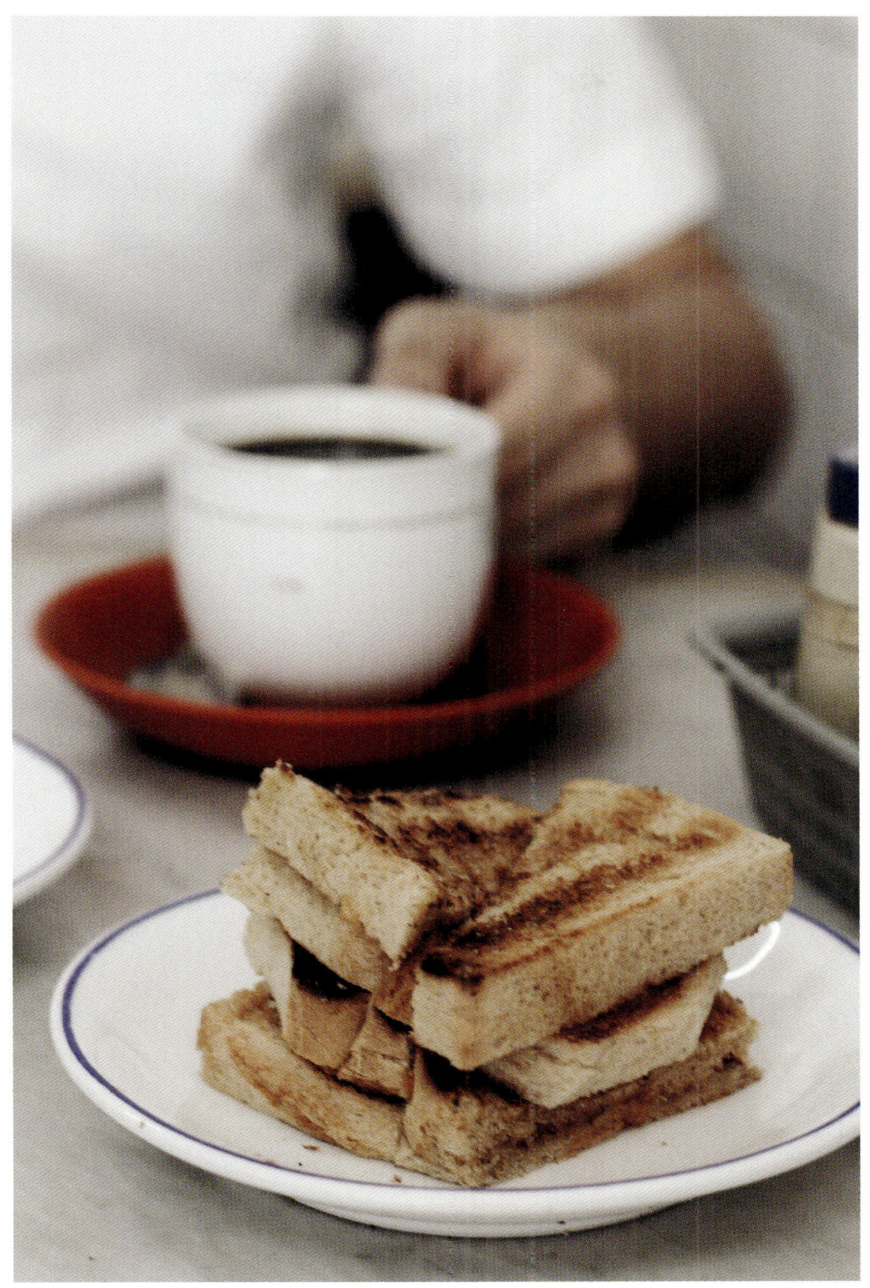

Saturday 10:45 AM                              Coffee break at Heap Seng Leong

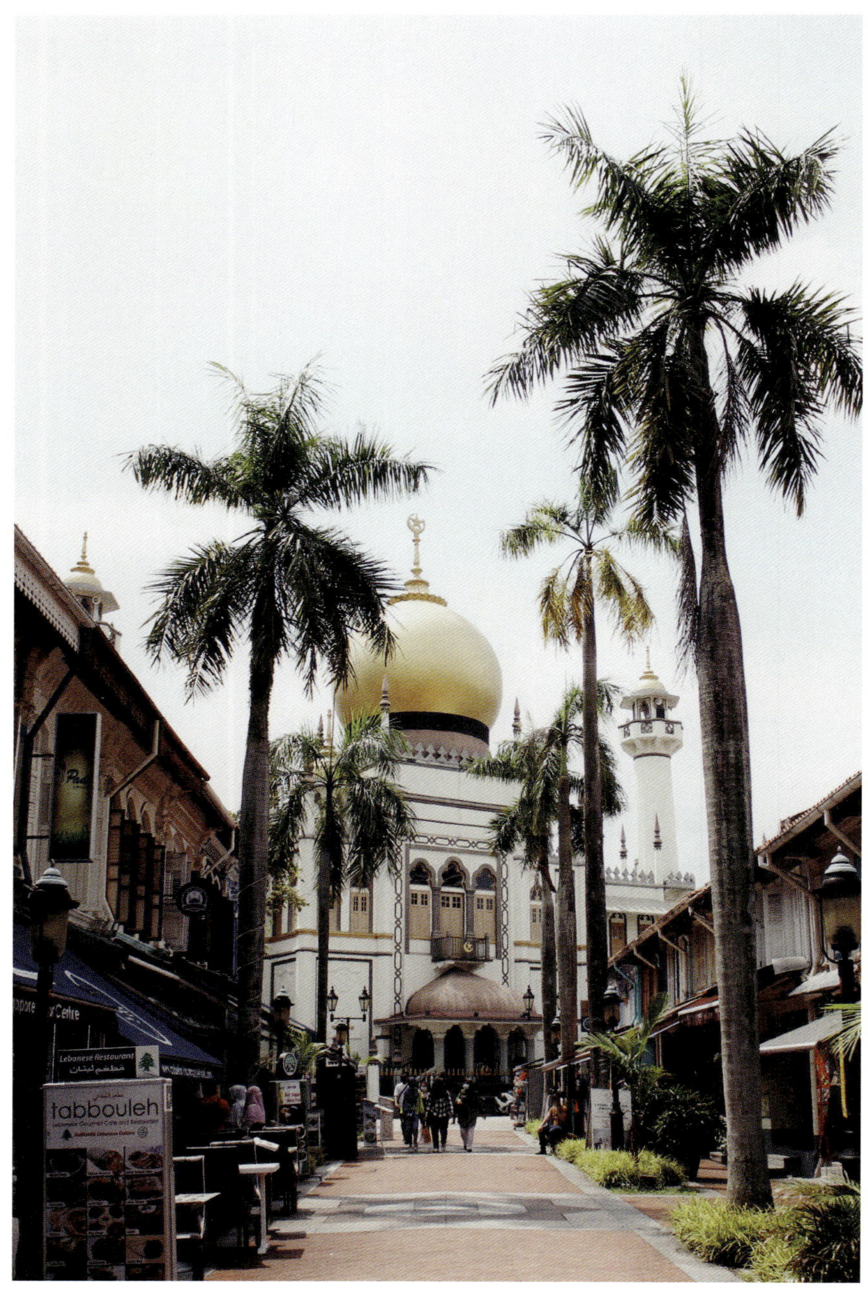

Lebanese Restaurant
tabbouleh

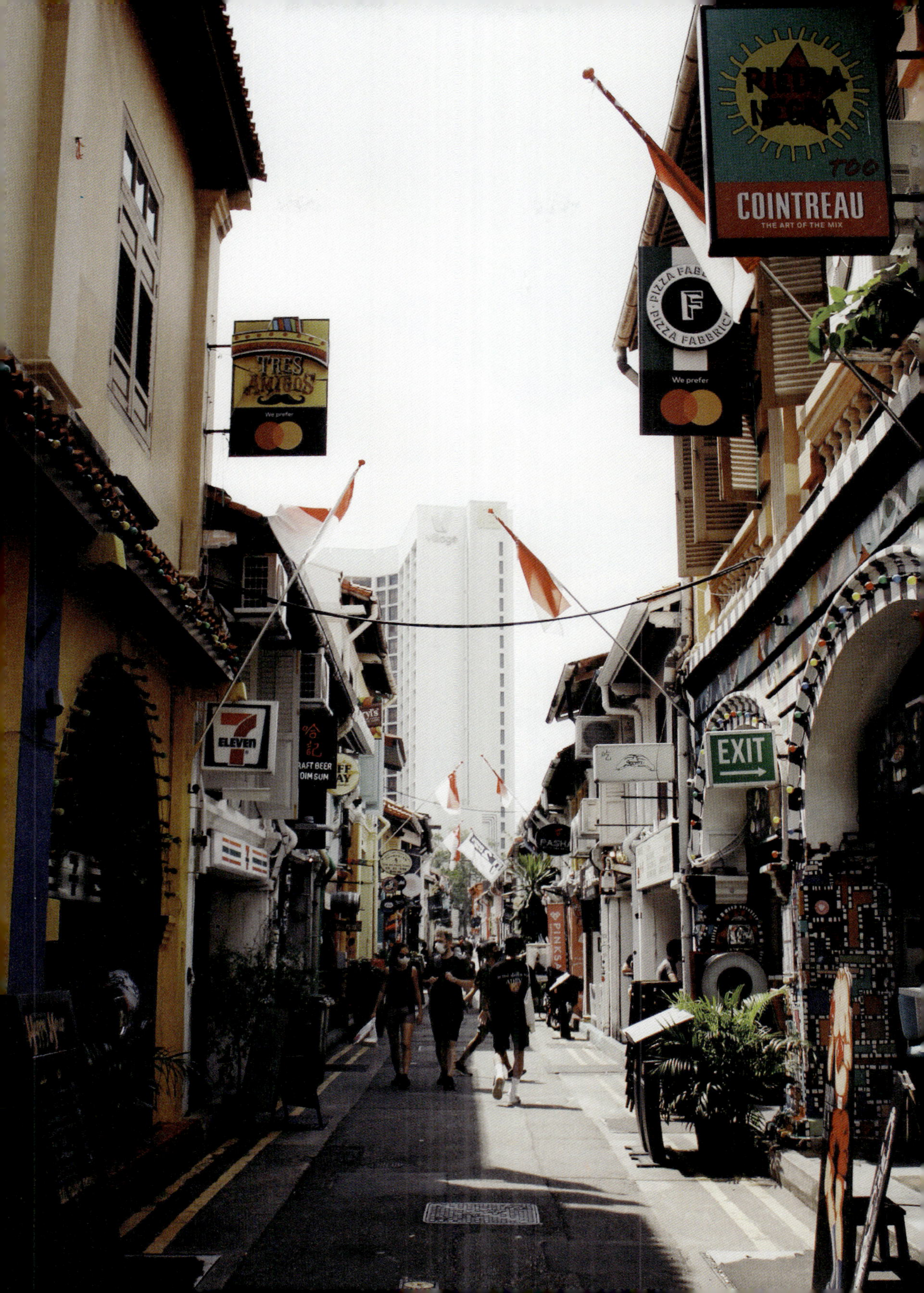

PIZZA NERA
COINTREAU
THE ART OF THE MIX
PIZZA FABBRICA
F
We prefer
TRES AMIGOS
We prefer
7 ELEVEN
哈記
CRAFT BEER
DIM SUN
EXIT
PINKS
吃记
FASH

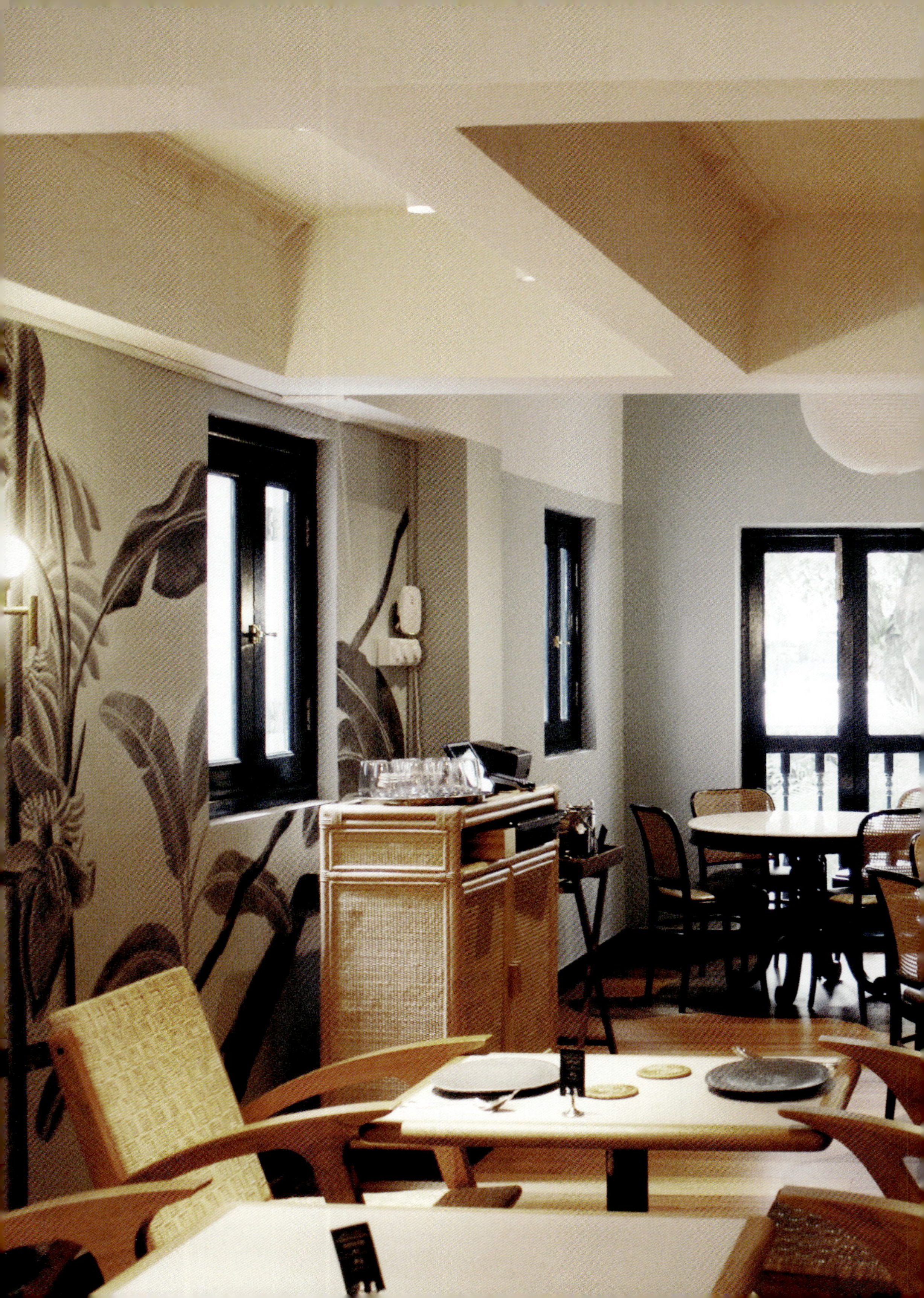

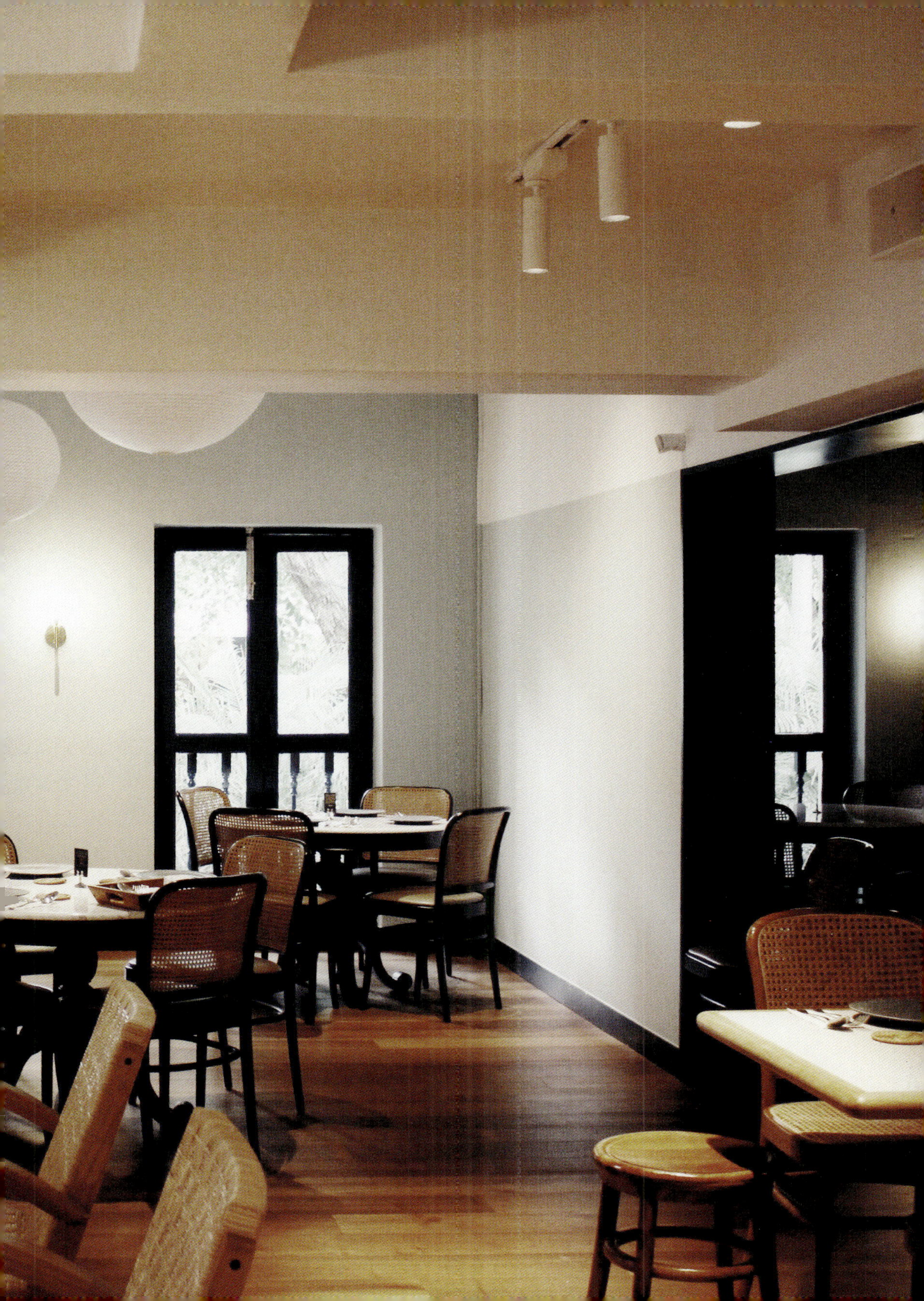

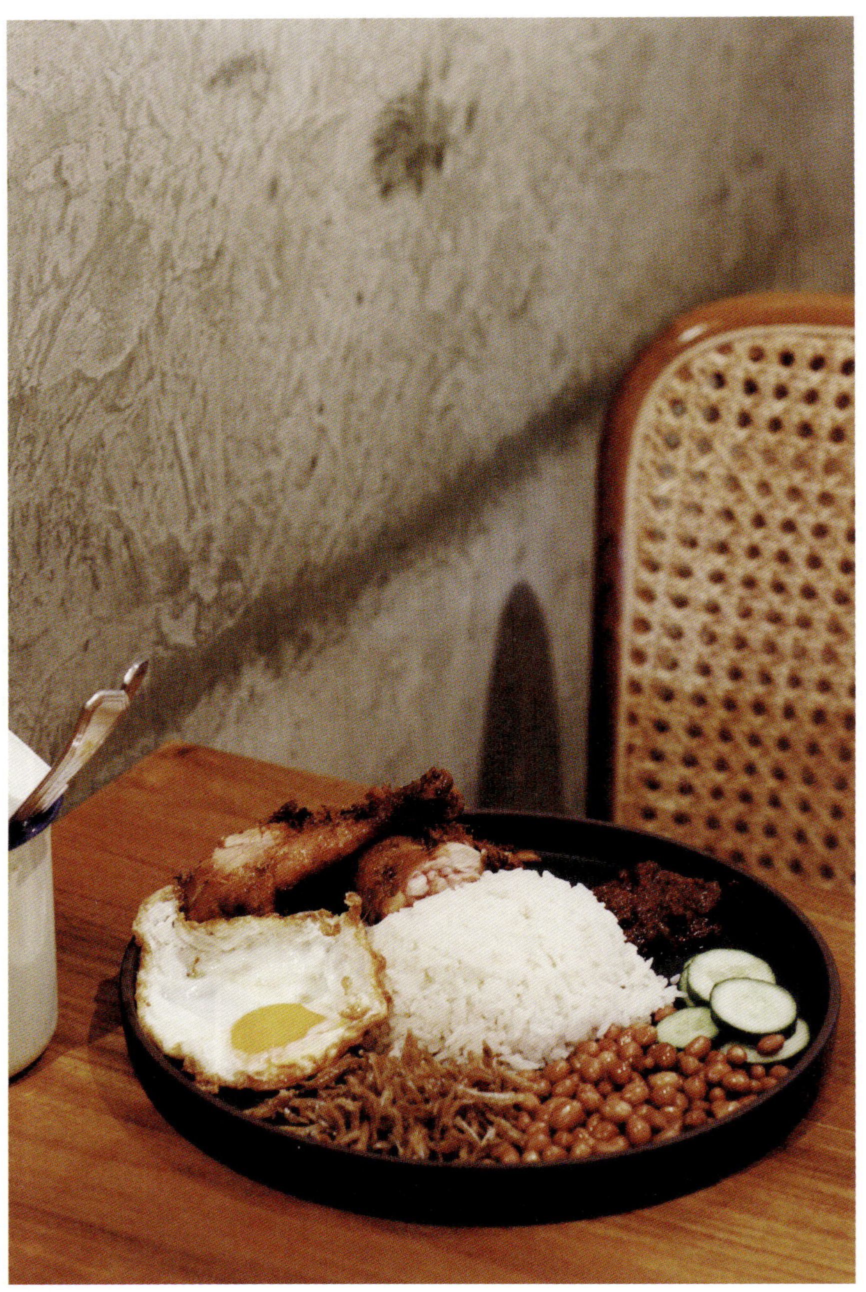

A late lunch at The Coconut Club

Saturday 1:25 PM

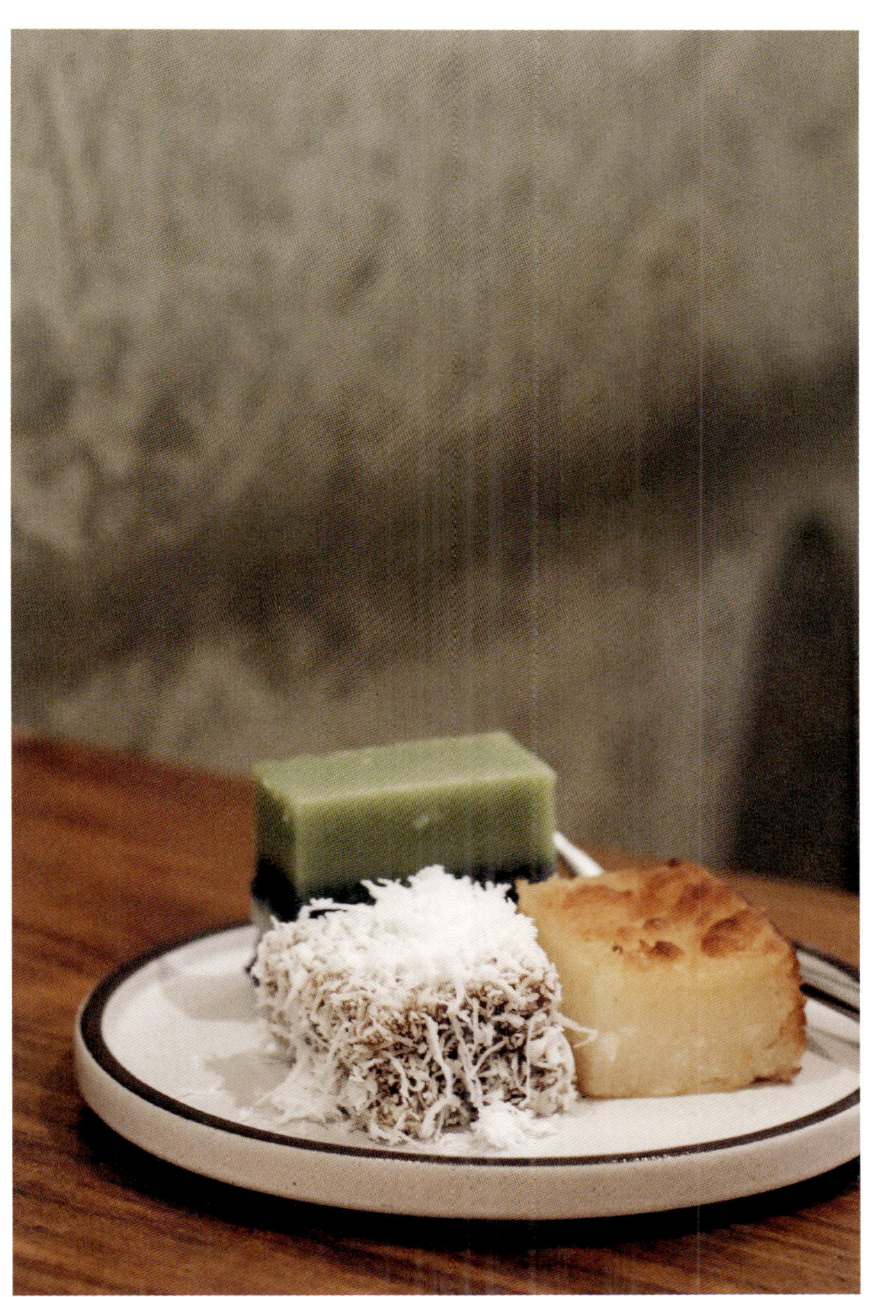

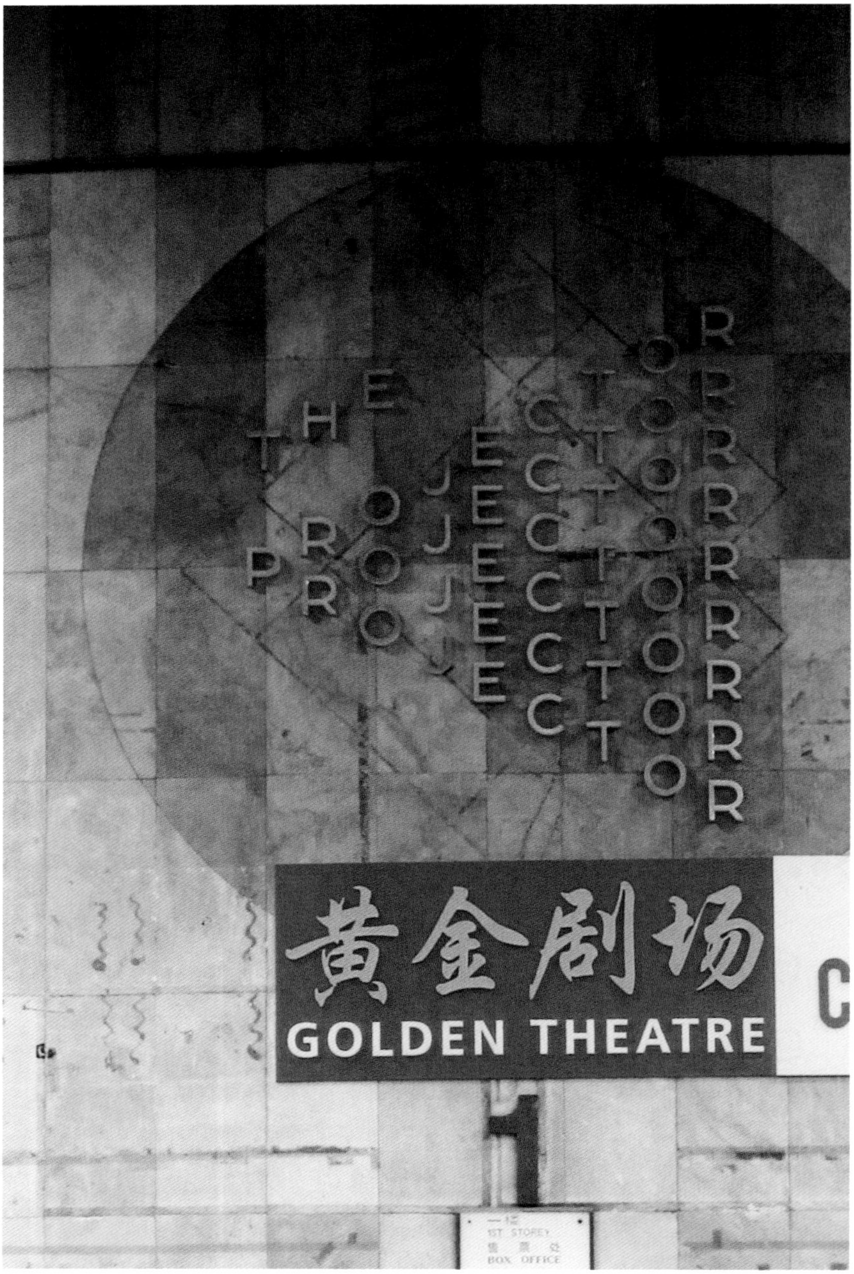

THE
PROJECTOR
PROJECTOR
PROJECTOR
PROJECTOR
PROJECTOR
PROJECTOR
PROJECTOR
黄金剧场
GOLDEN THEATRE
C
一楼
1ST STOREY
售票处
BOX OFFICE

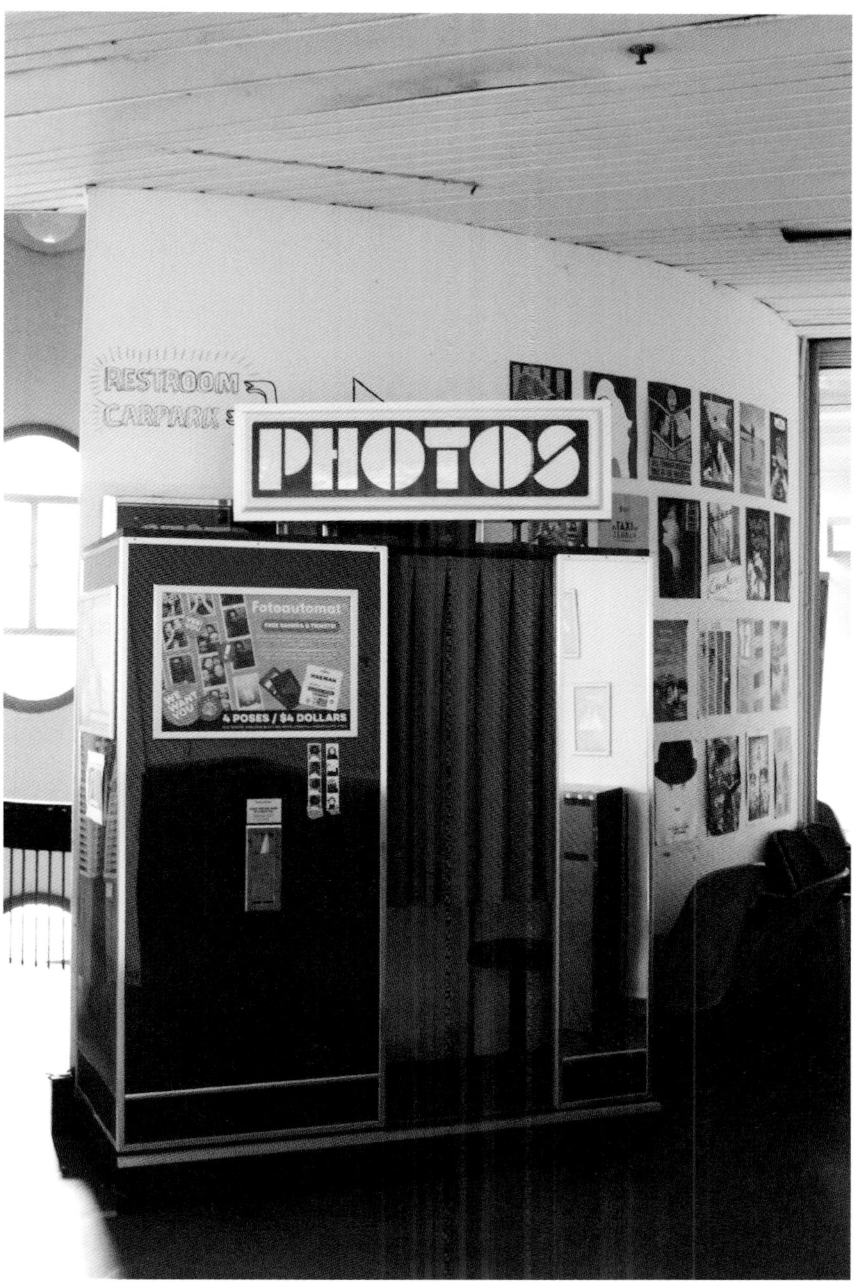




Catching a film at The Projector

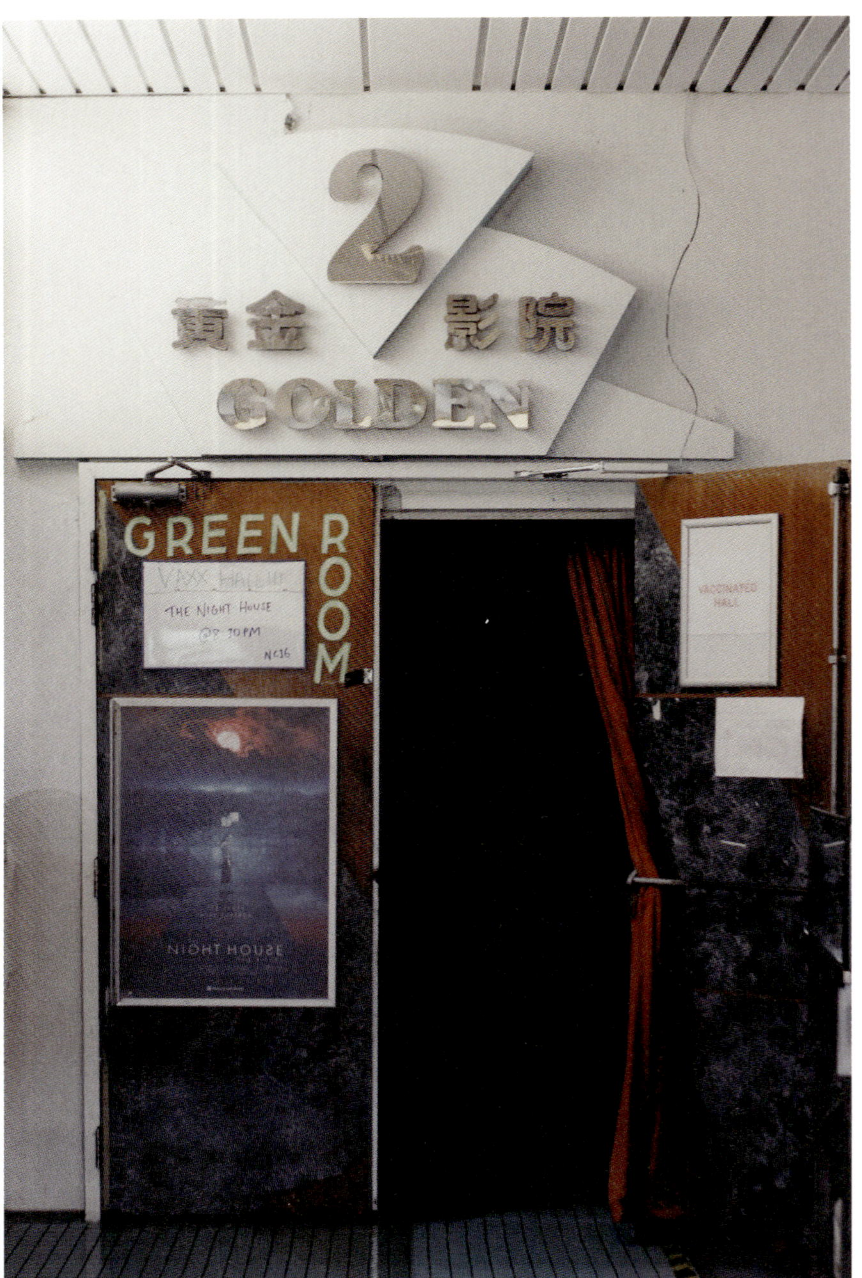

2
黃金　影院
GOLDEN
GREEN ROOM
VAXX HALL?
THE NIGHT HOUSE
@8:30PM
NC16
NIGHT HOUSE
VACCINATED
HALL

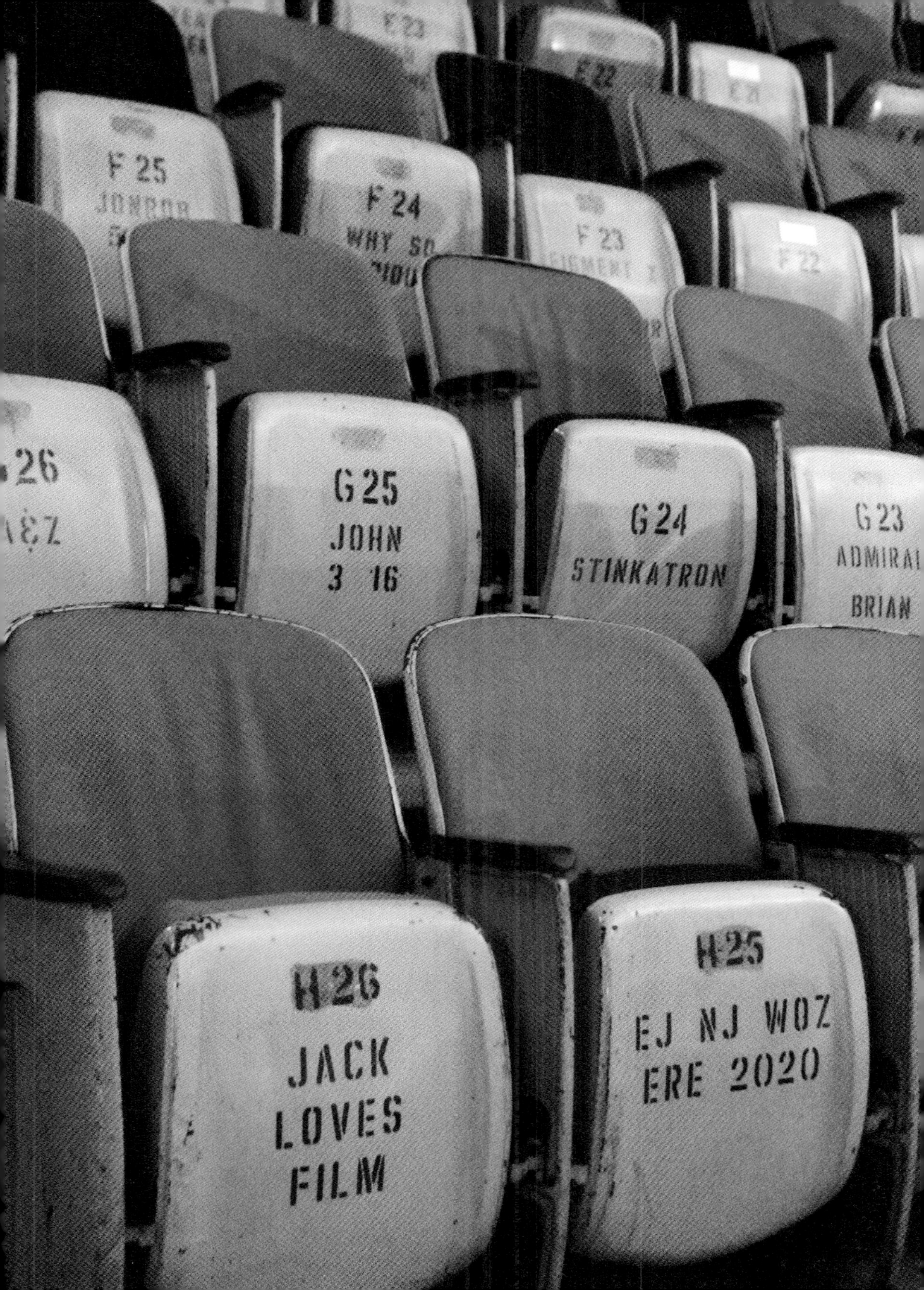

F 25
JONROB
F 24
WHY SO
RIOU
F 23
IGMENT
F 22
26
&Z
G 25
JOHN
3 16
G 24
STINKATRON
G 23
ADMIRAL
BRIAN
H 26
JACK
LOVES
FILM
H 25
EJ NJ WOZ
ERE 2020

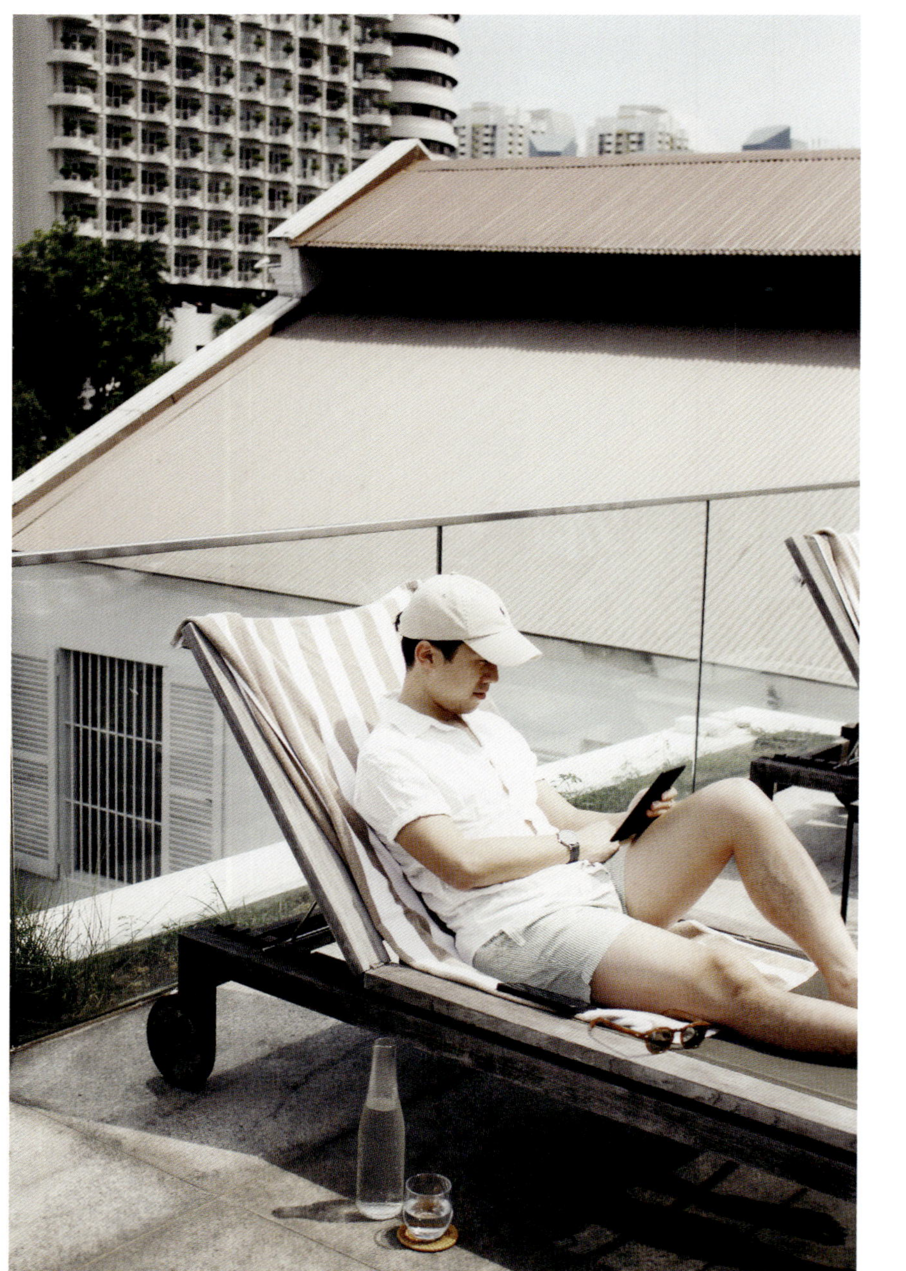

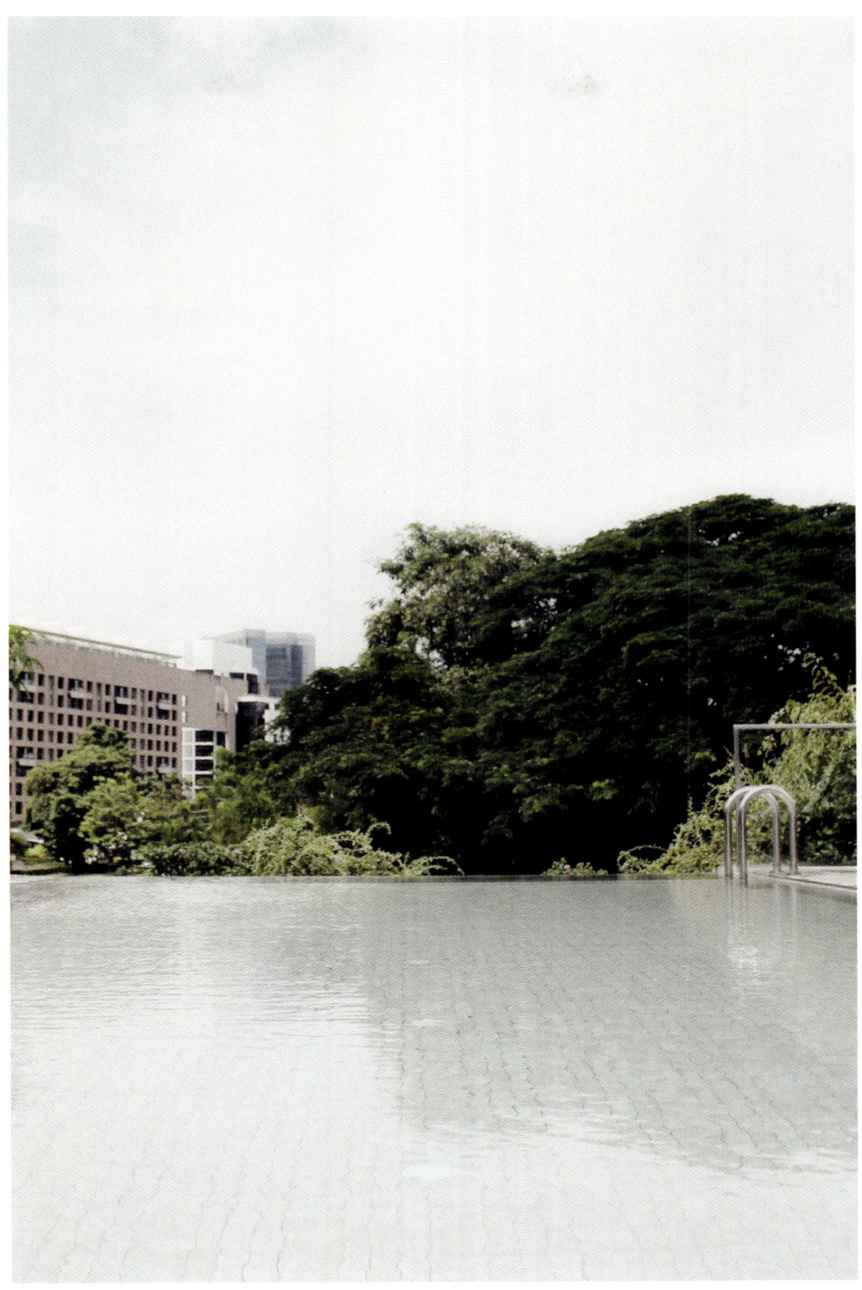

Saturday 5:30 PMWinding down by the pool

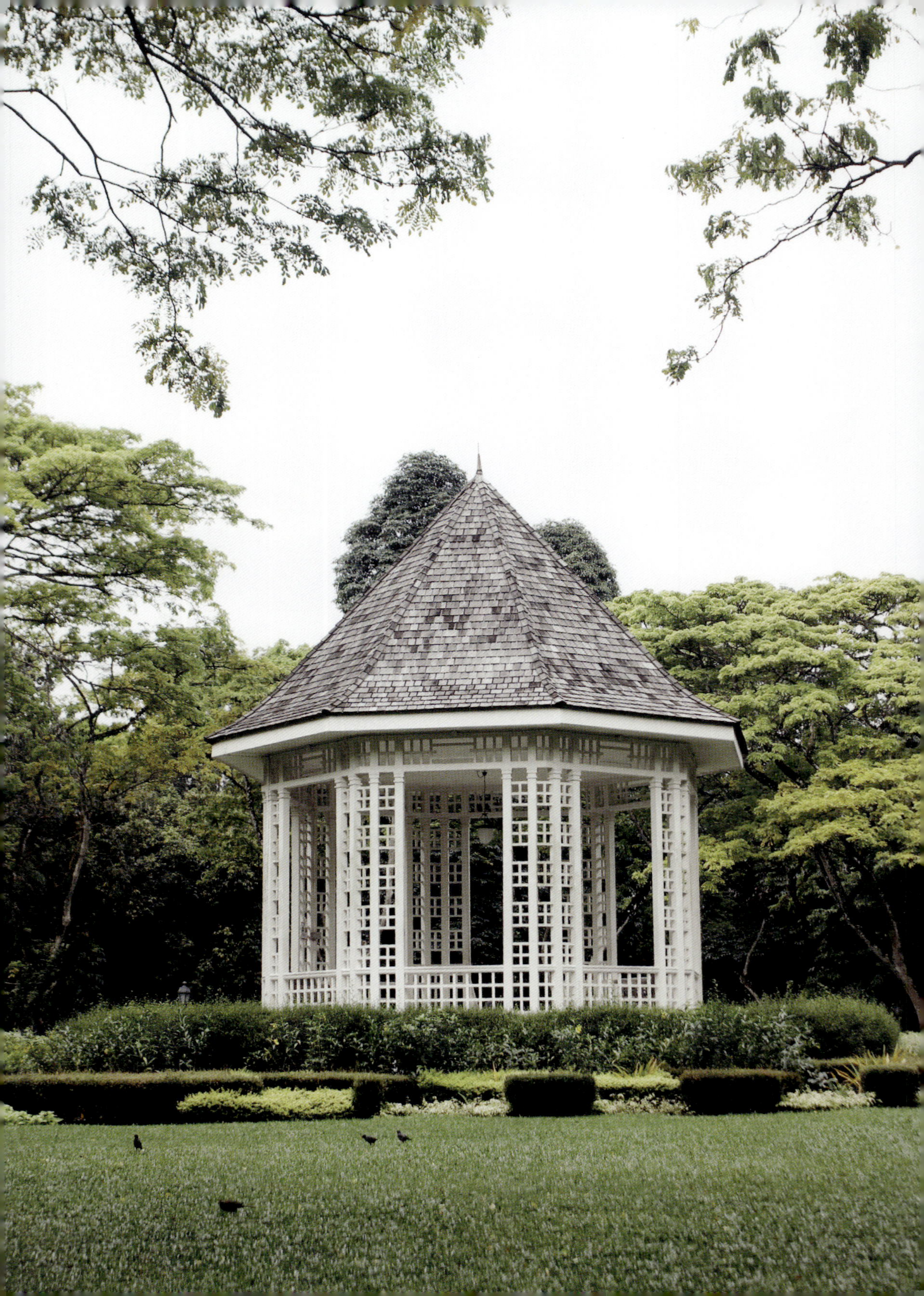

Sunday

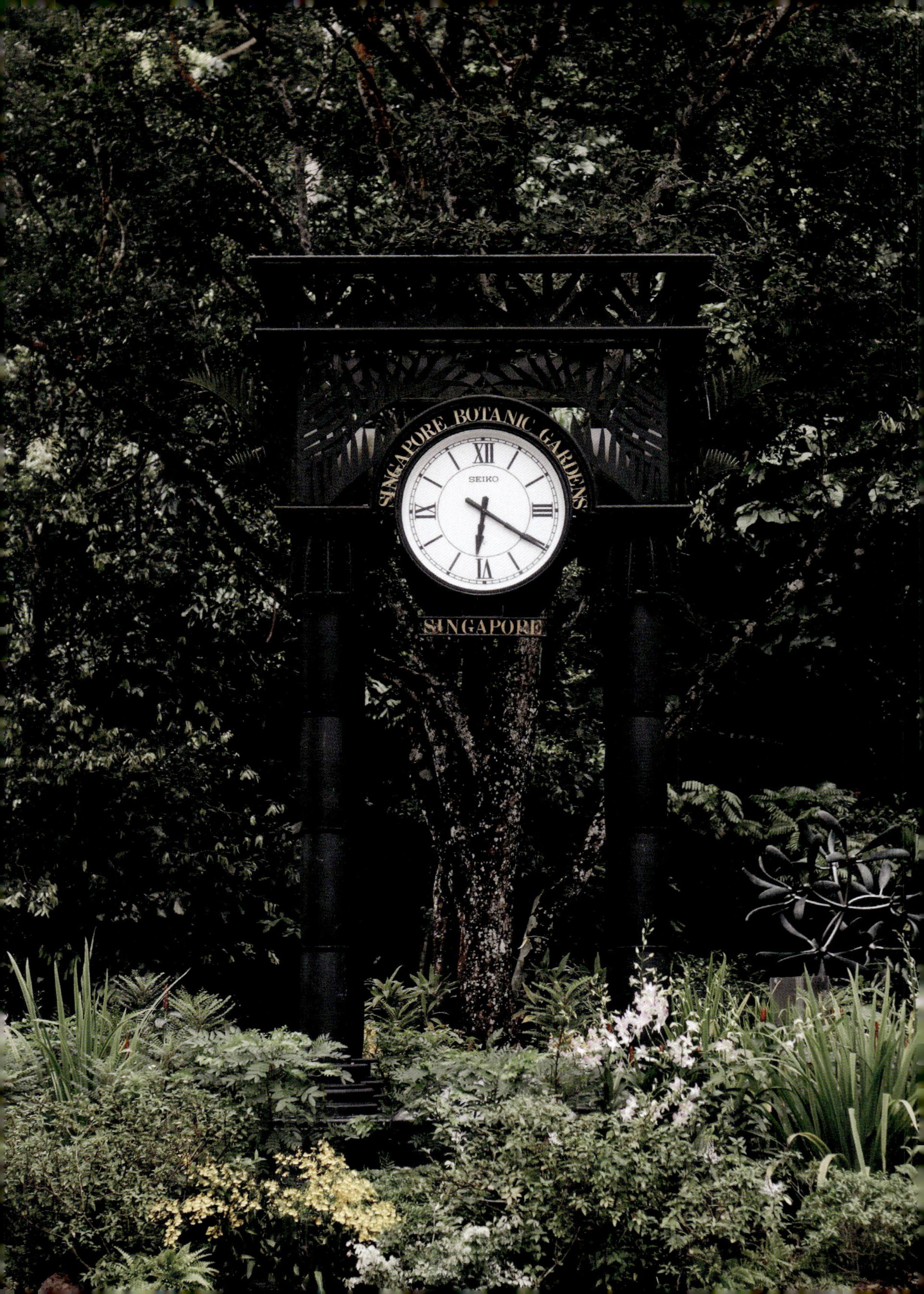

SINGAPORE BOTANIC GARDENS
SEIKO
SINGAPORE

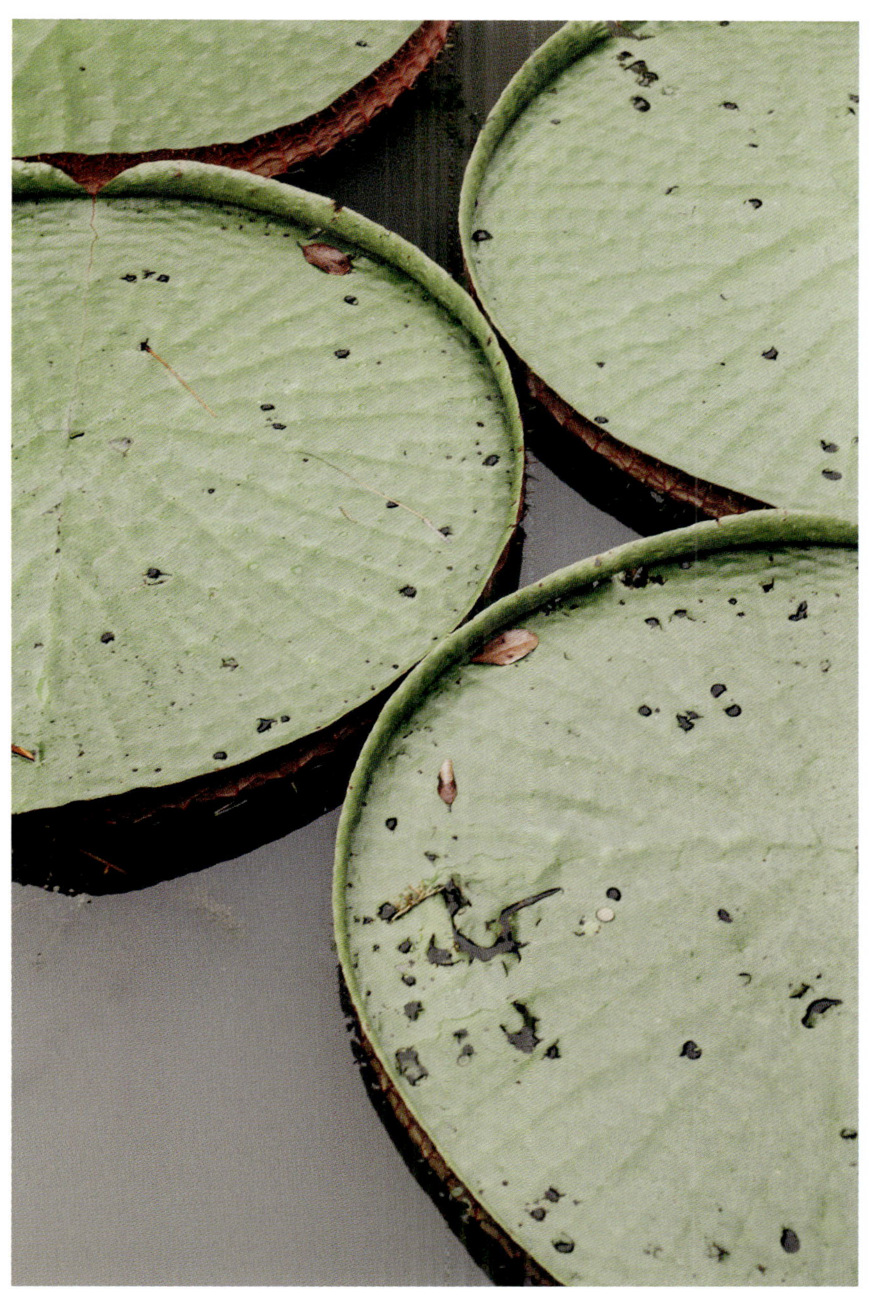

Sunday 9:05 AM                    Morning walk in the Botanical Gardens

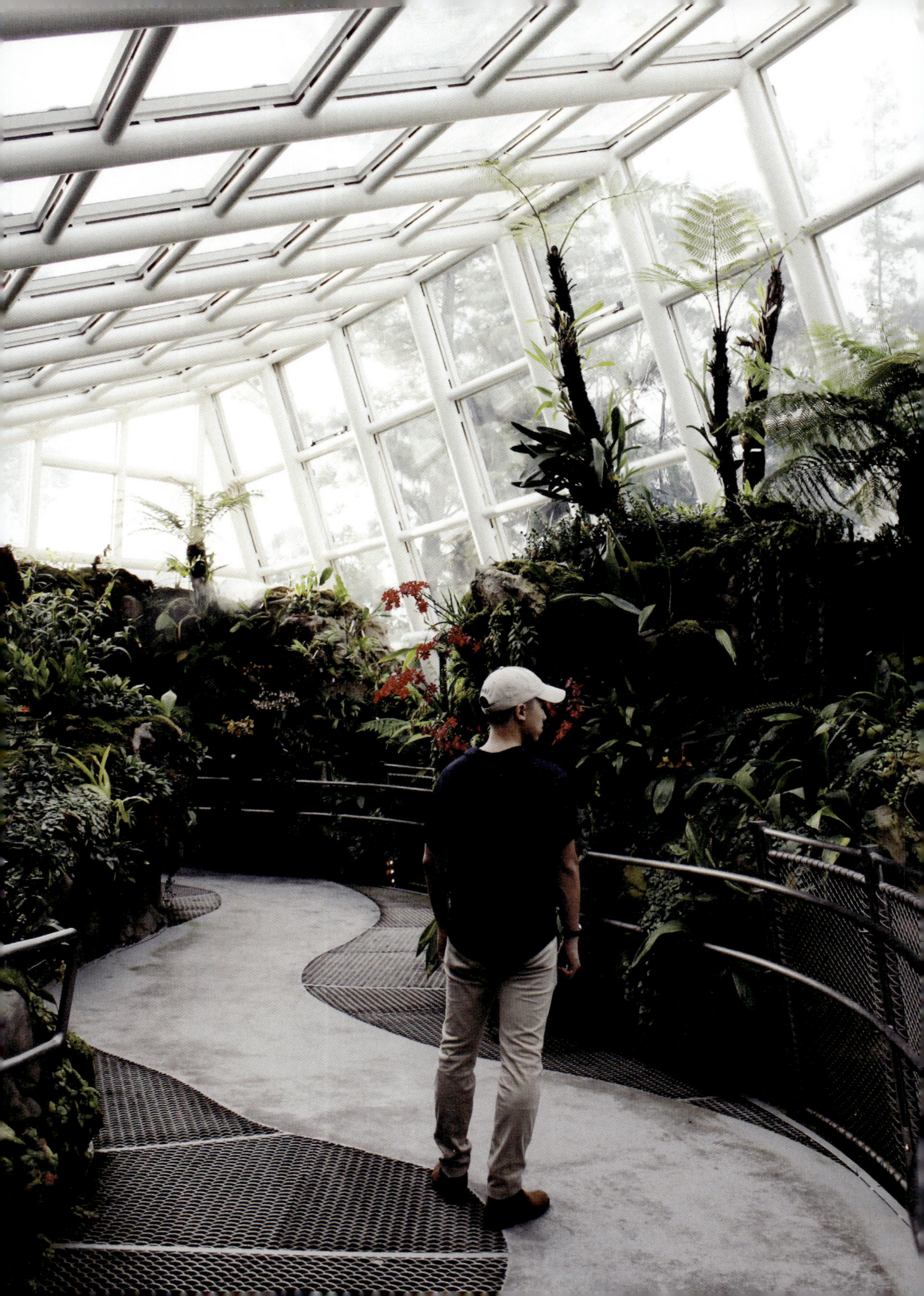

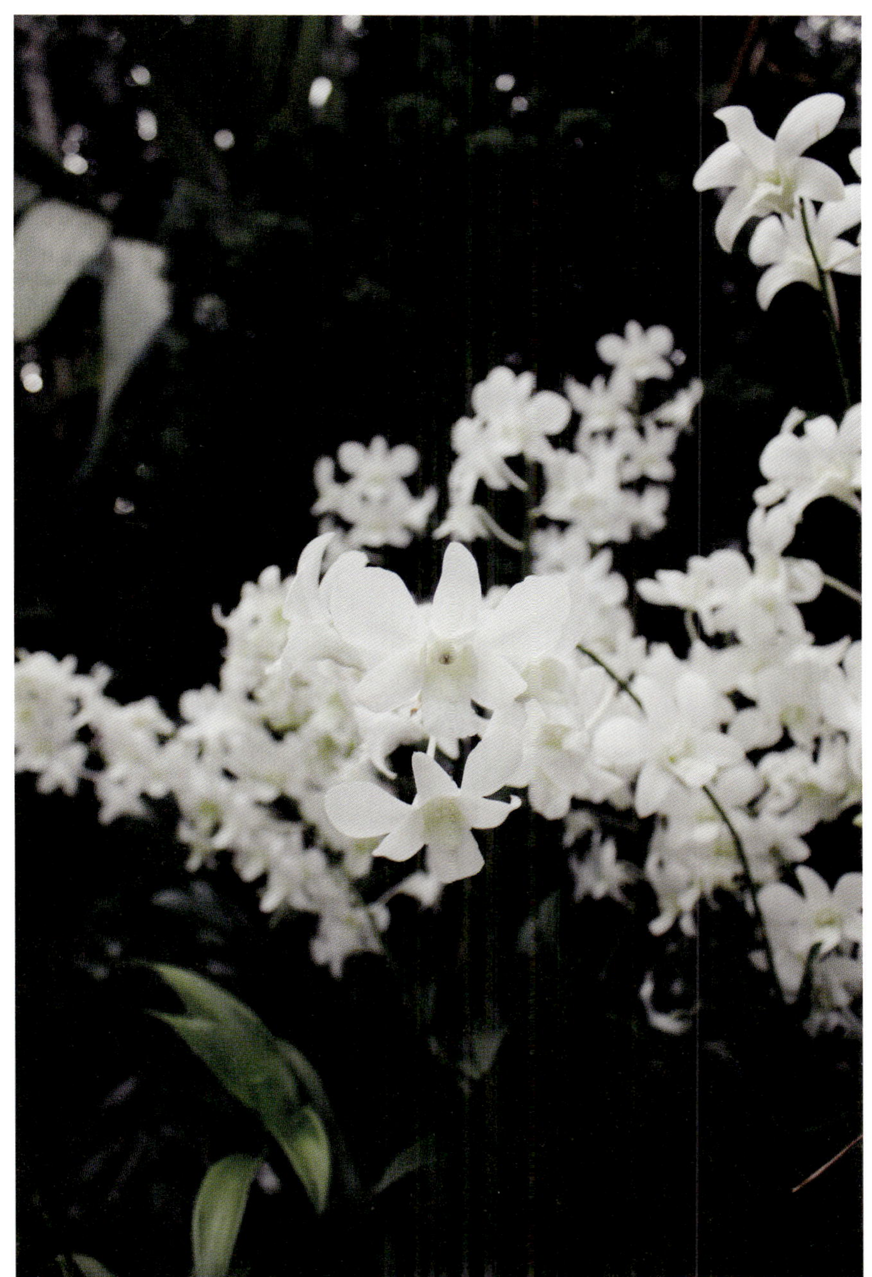

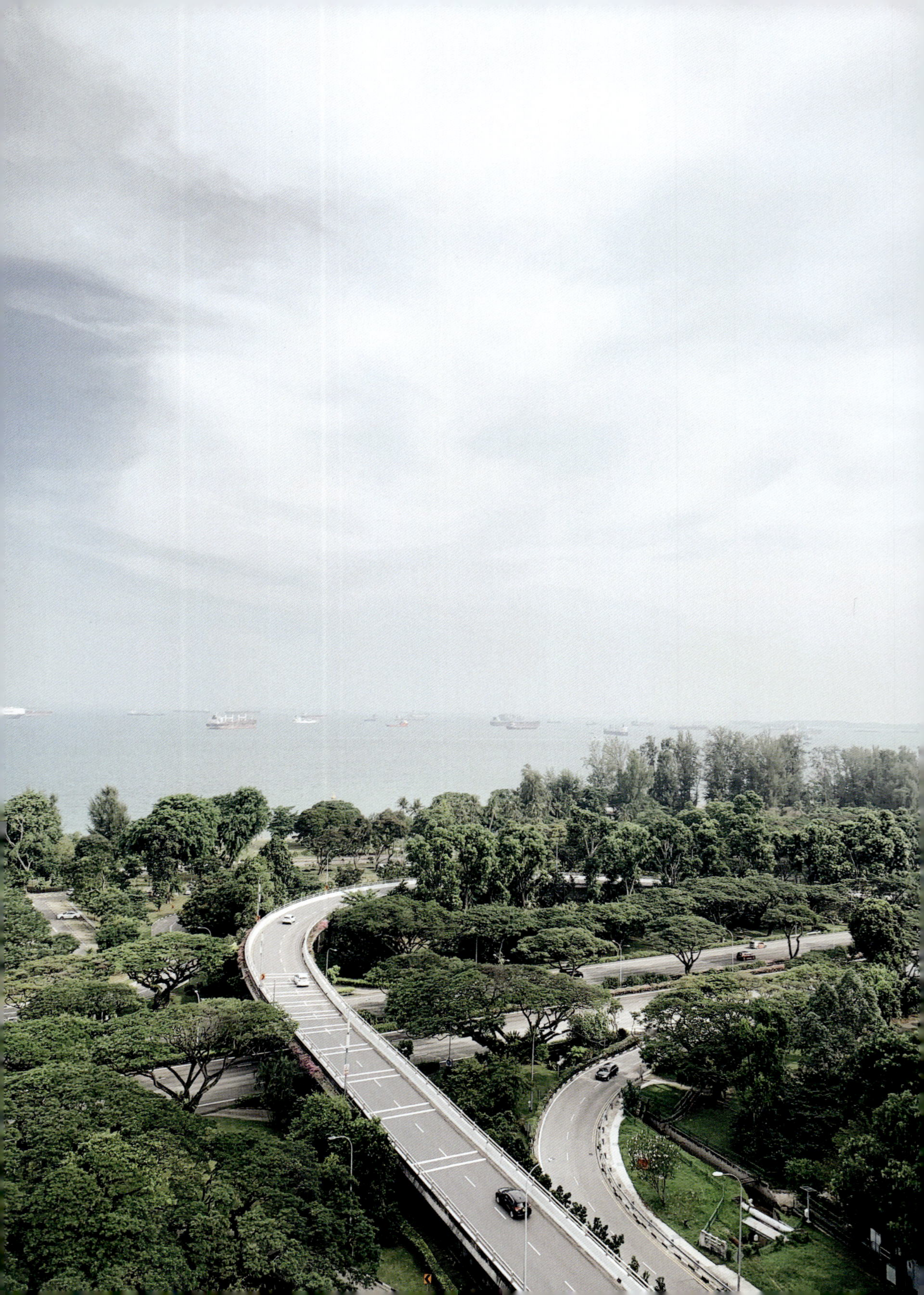

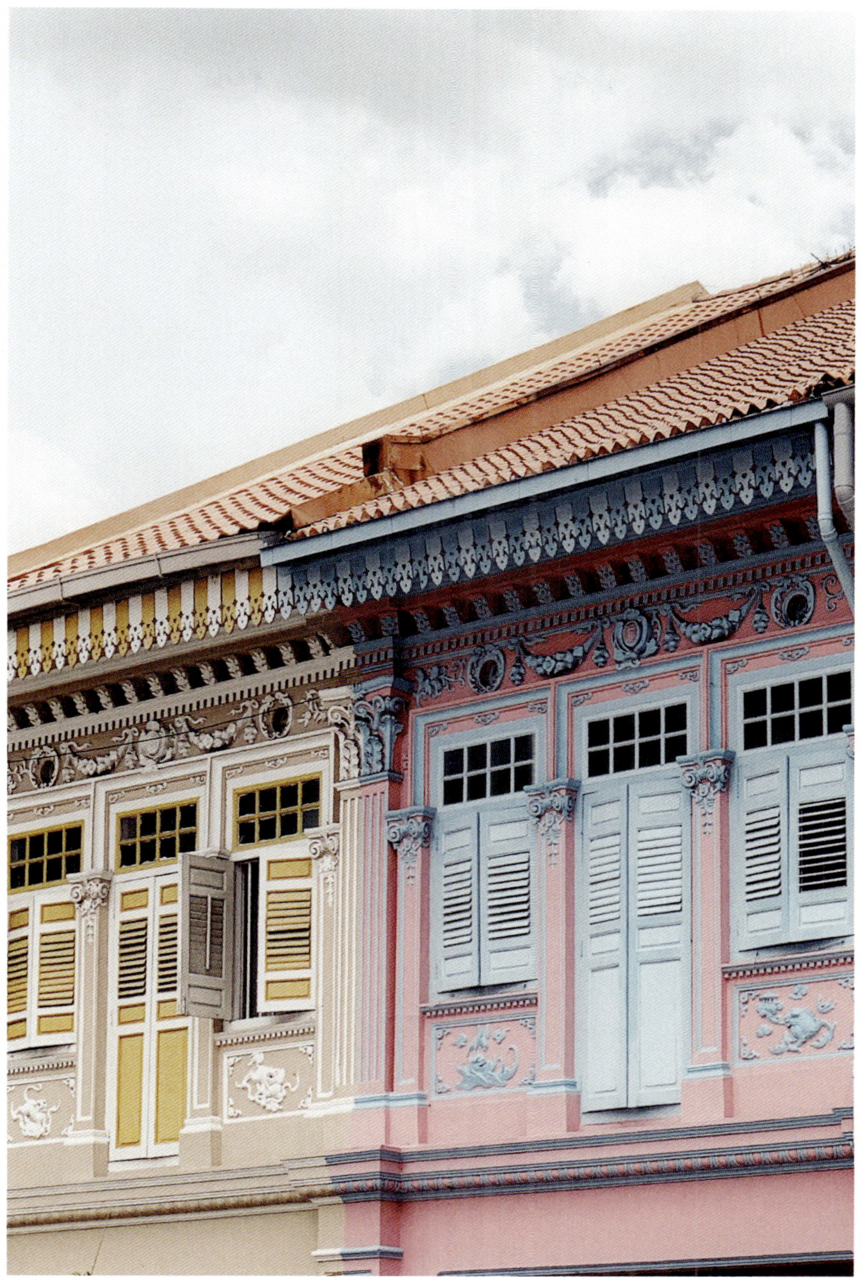

Sunday 11:15 AM                              Traditional 'Peranakan' houses in Joo Chiat

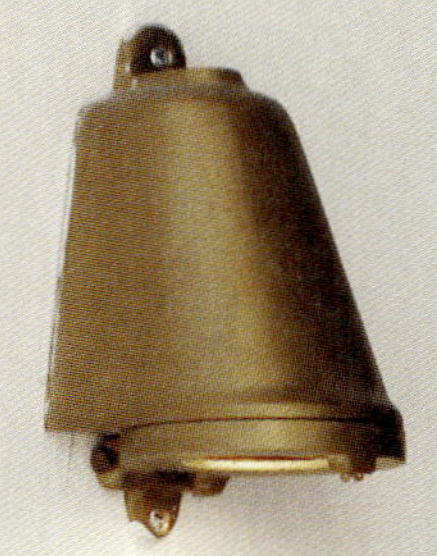
SOJAO

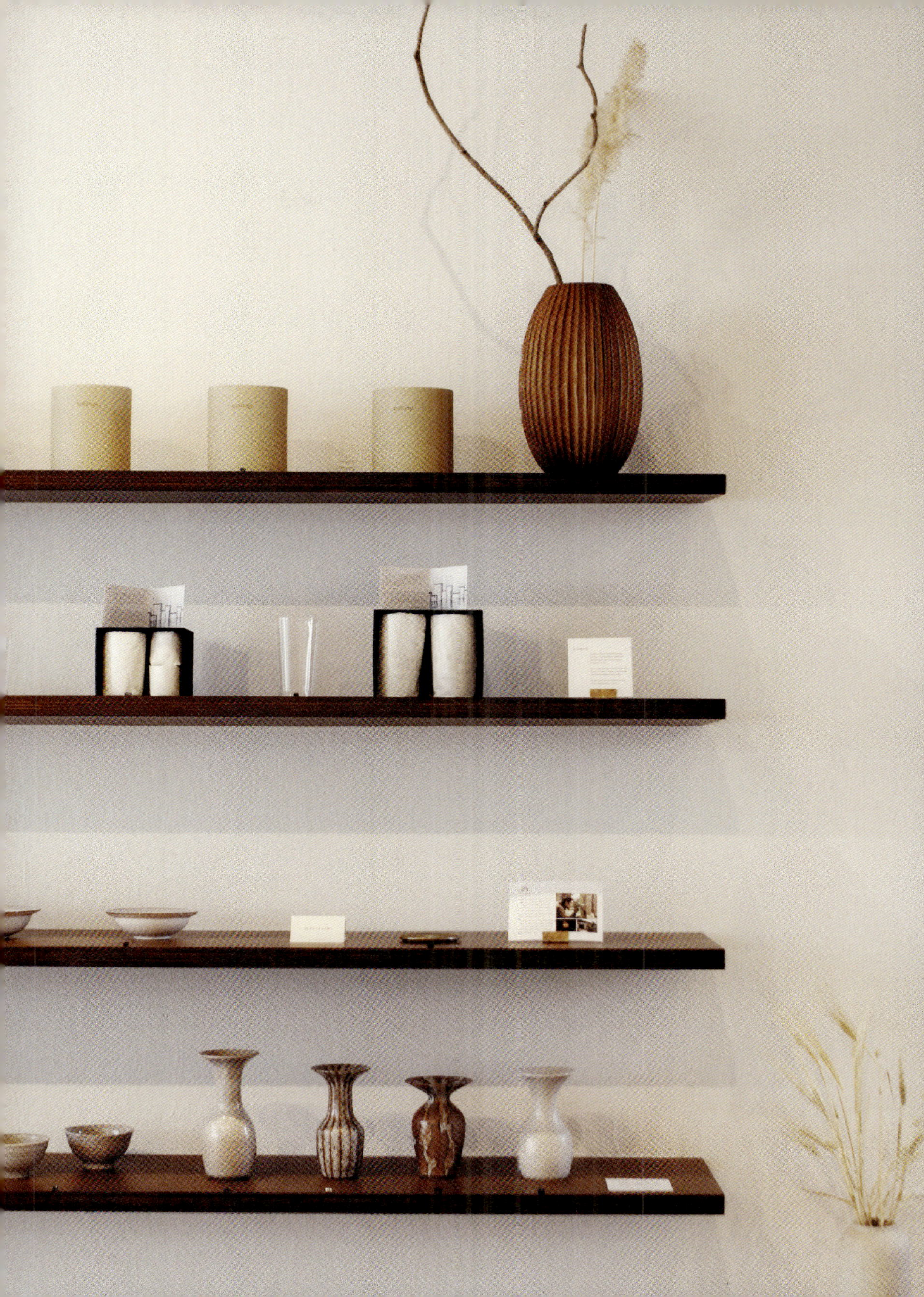

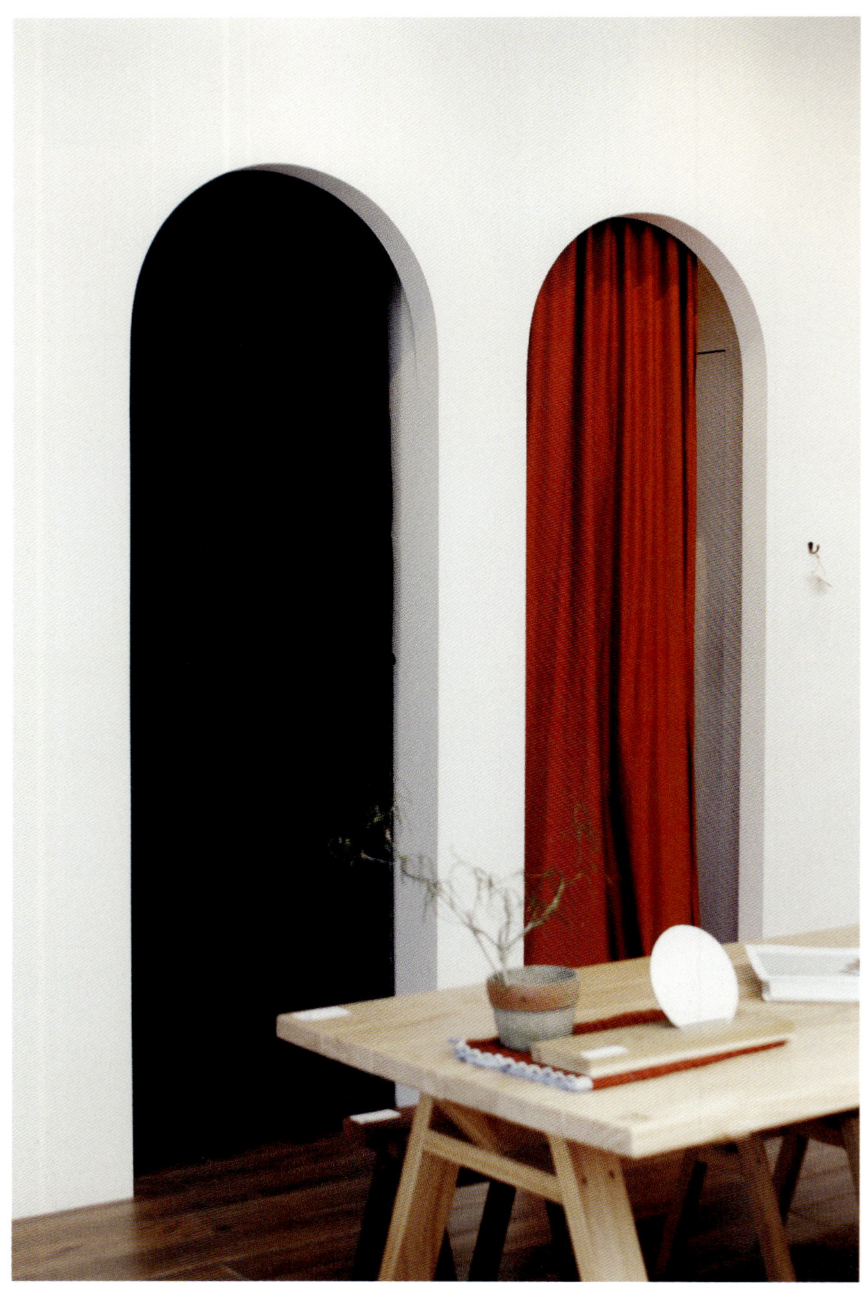

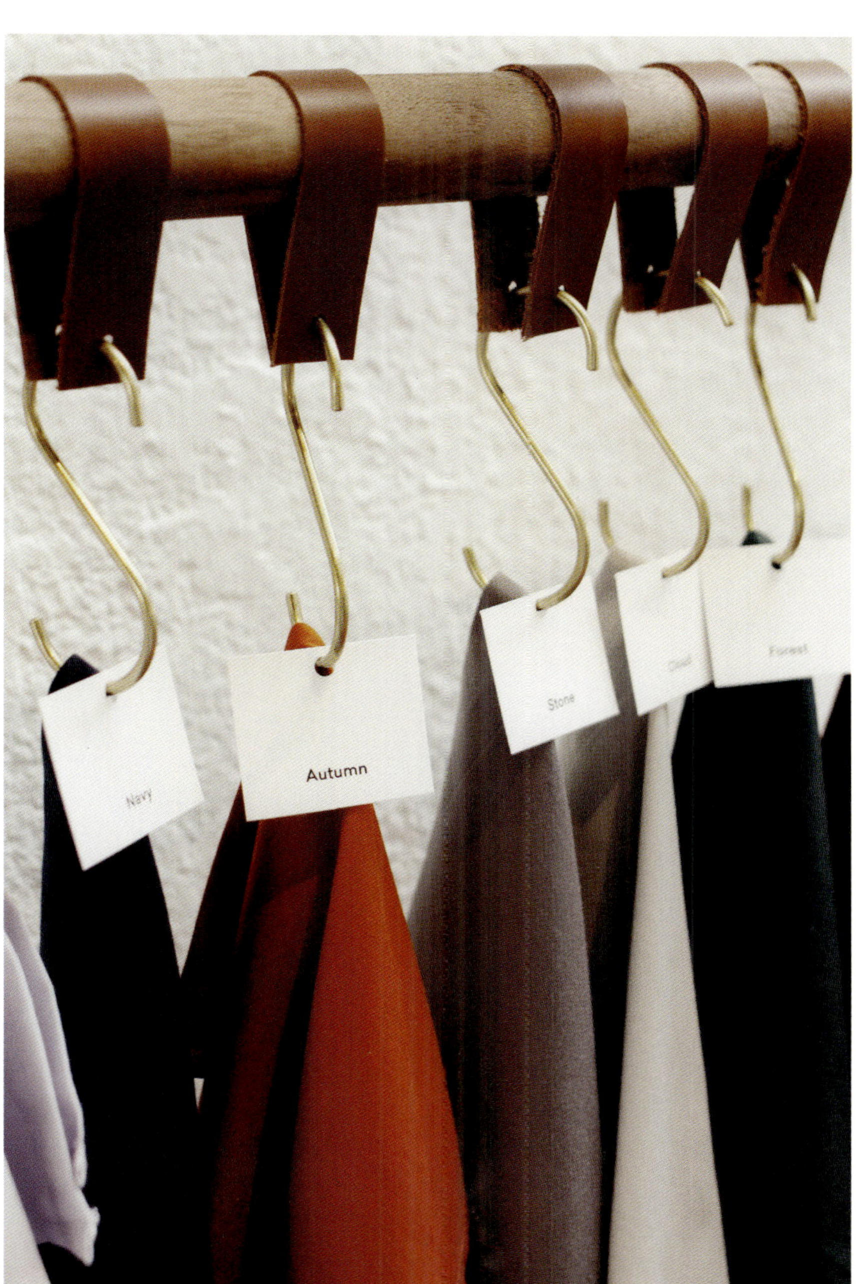
Navy
Autumn
Stone
Oak
Forest

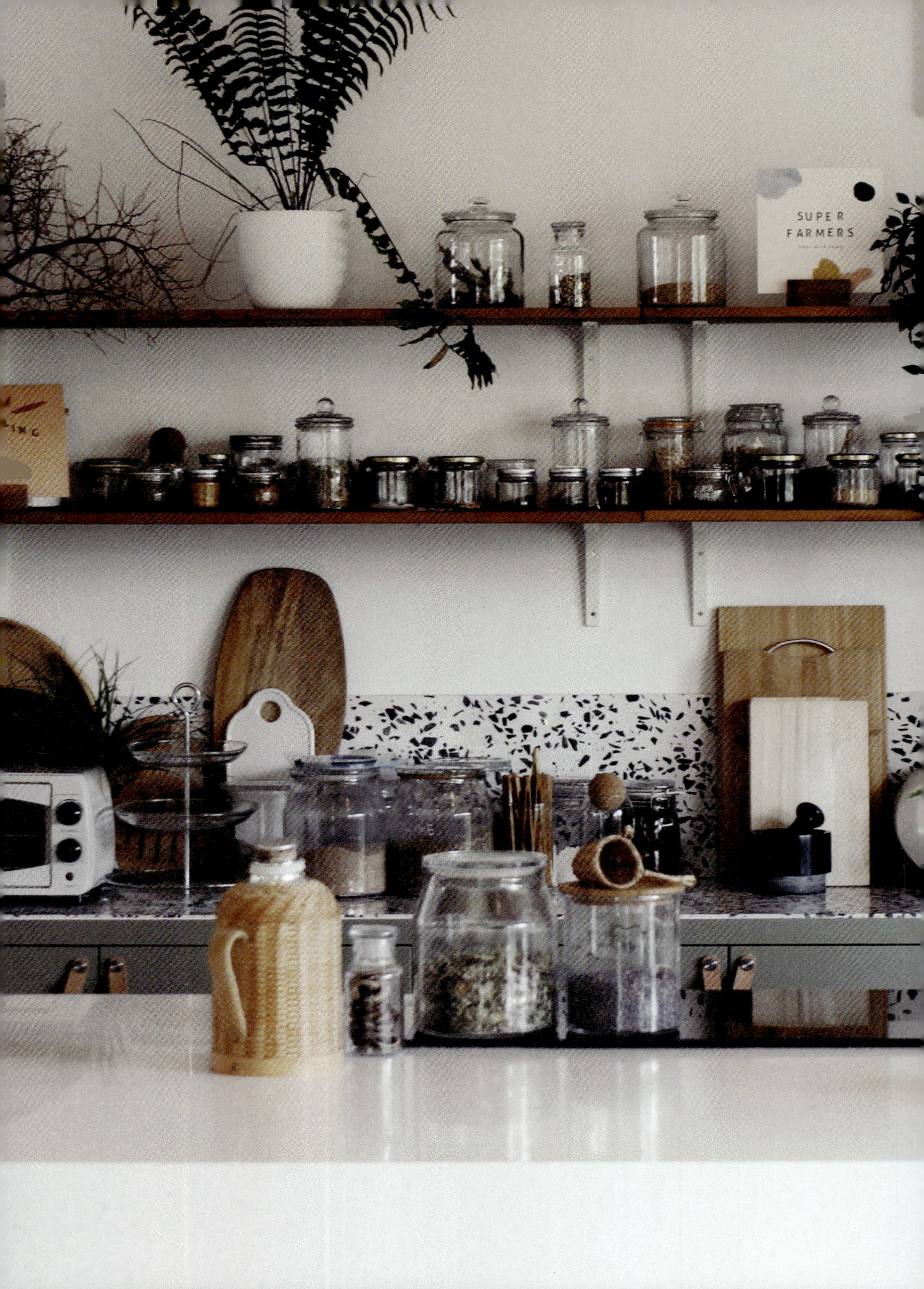
SUPER
FARMERS

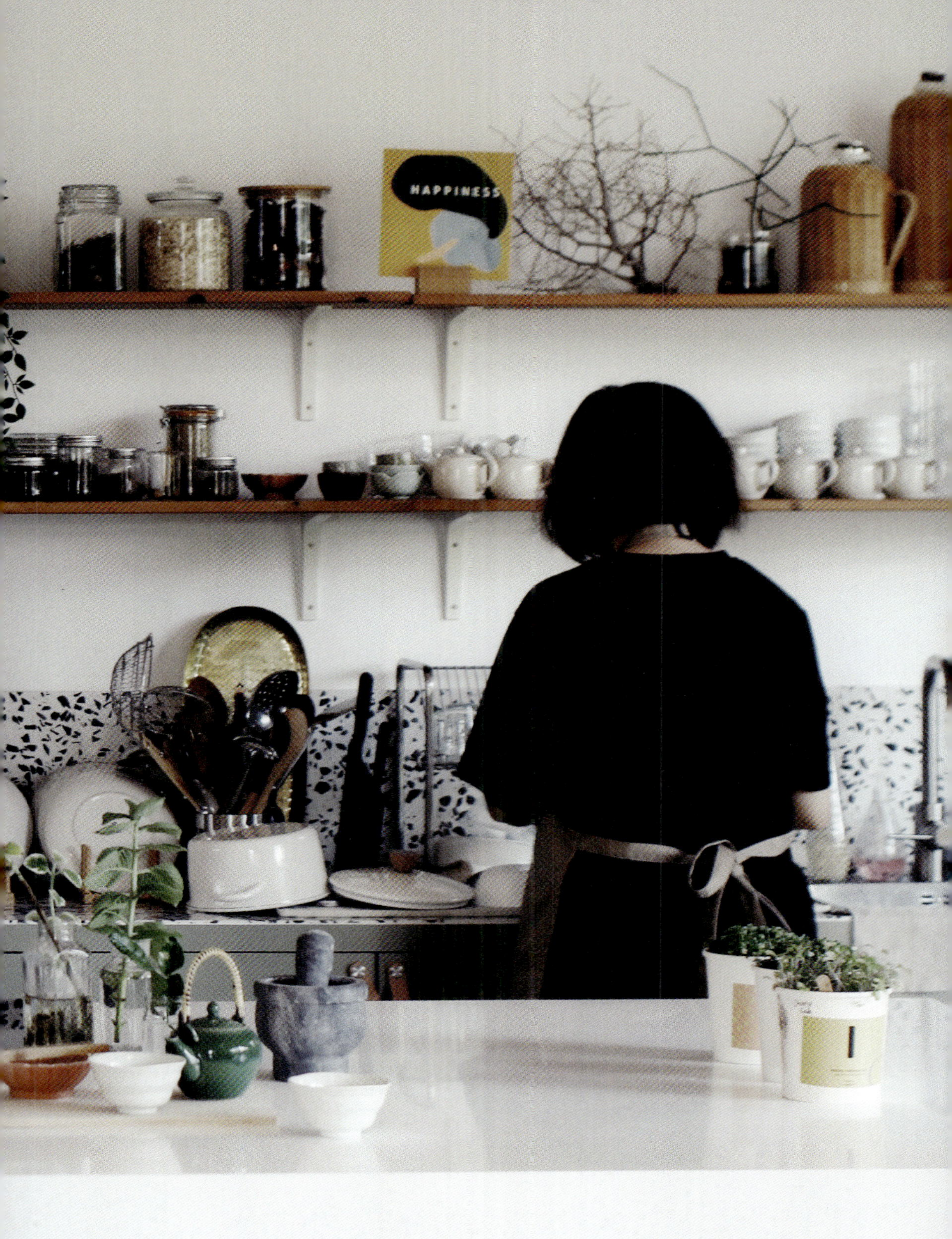
HAPPINESS

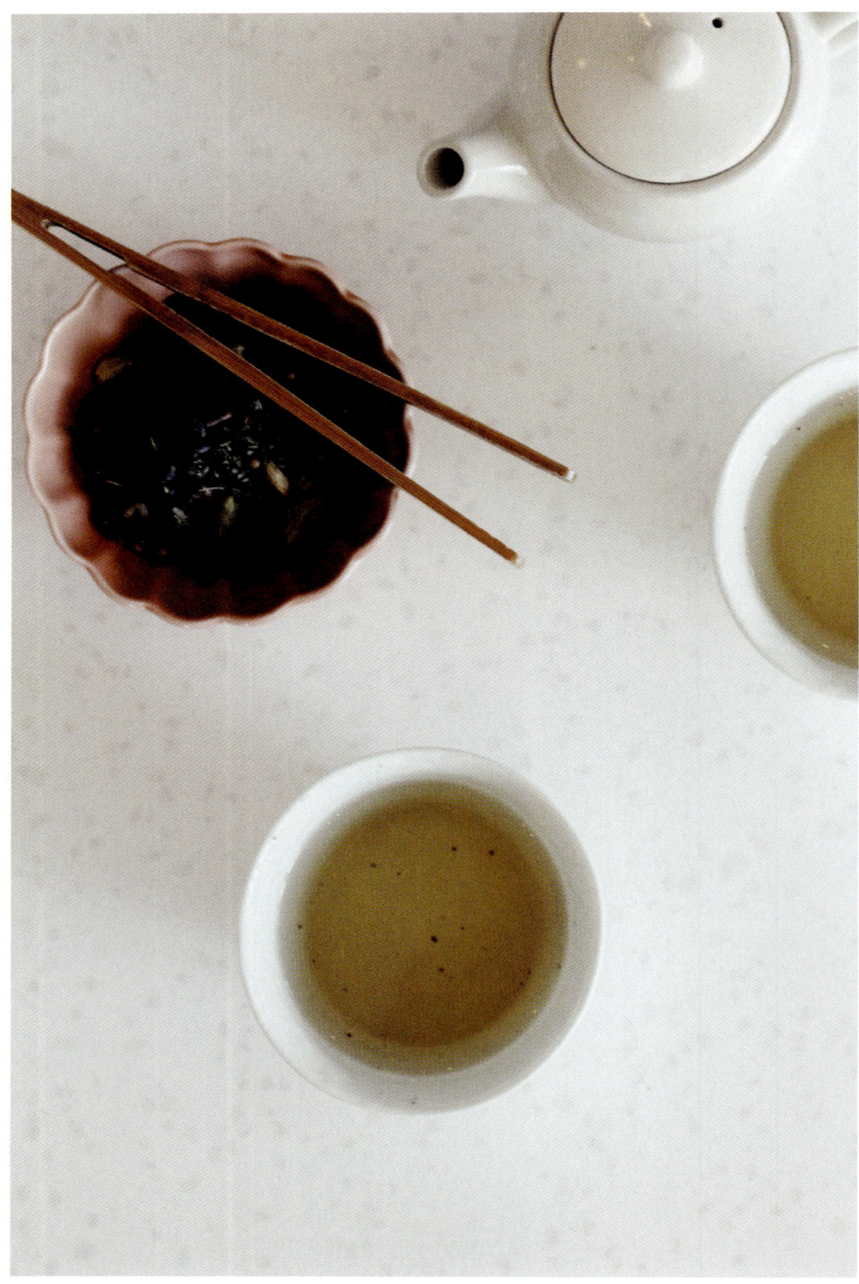

Tea workshop at Superfarmers                    Sunday 12:00 PM

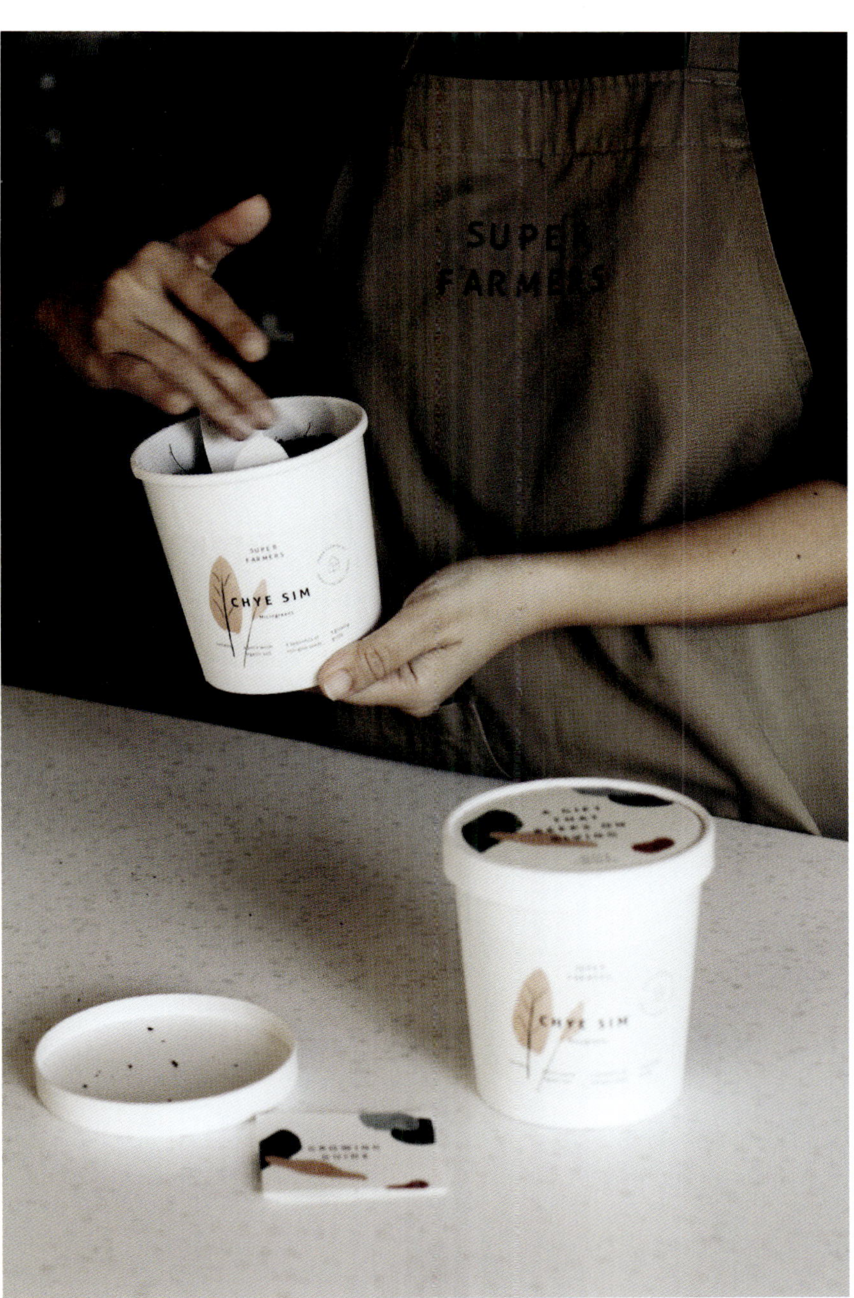

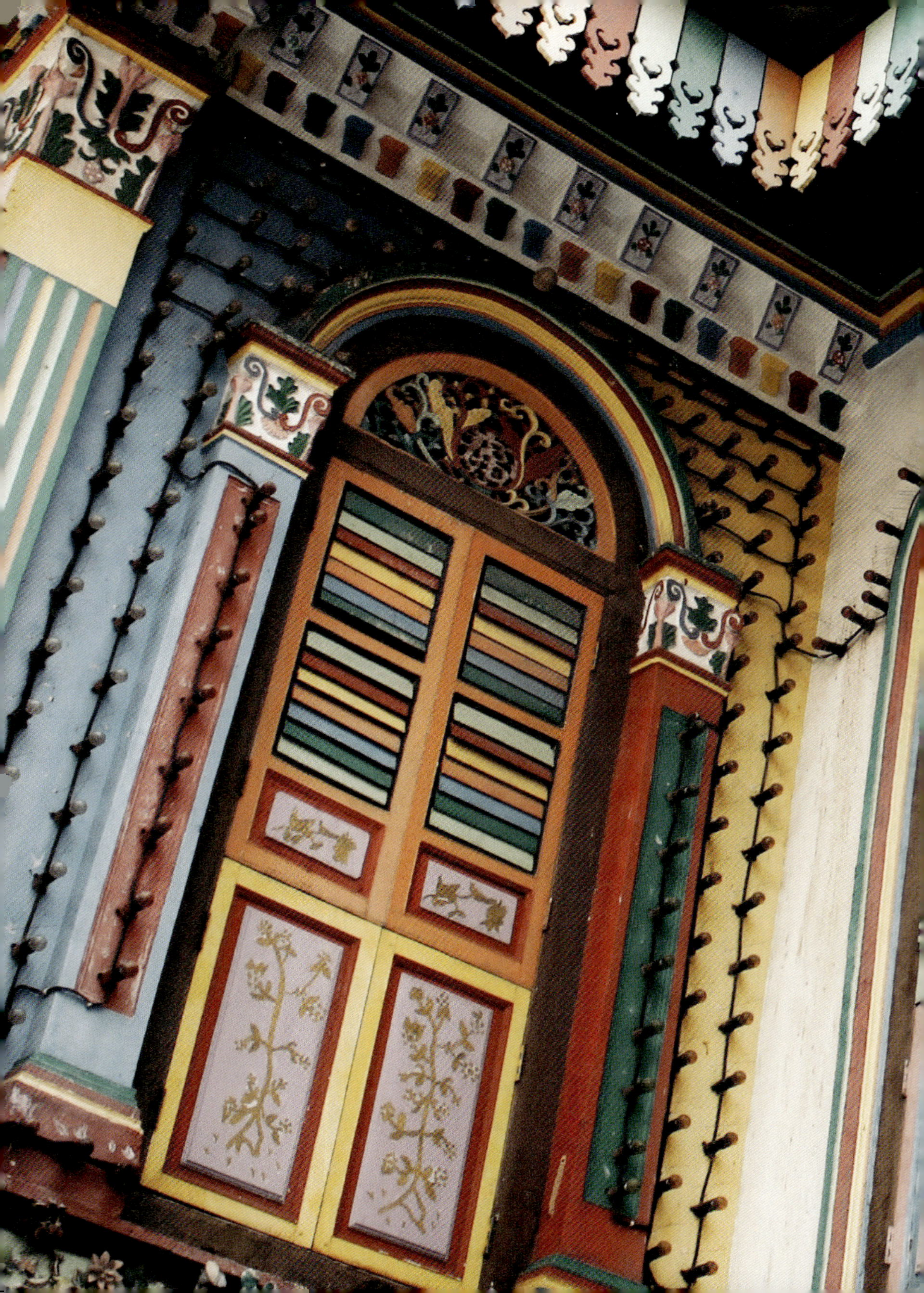

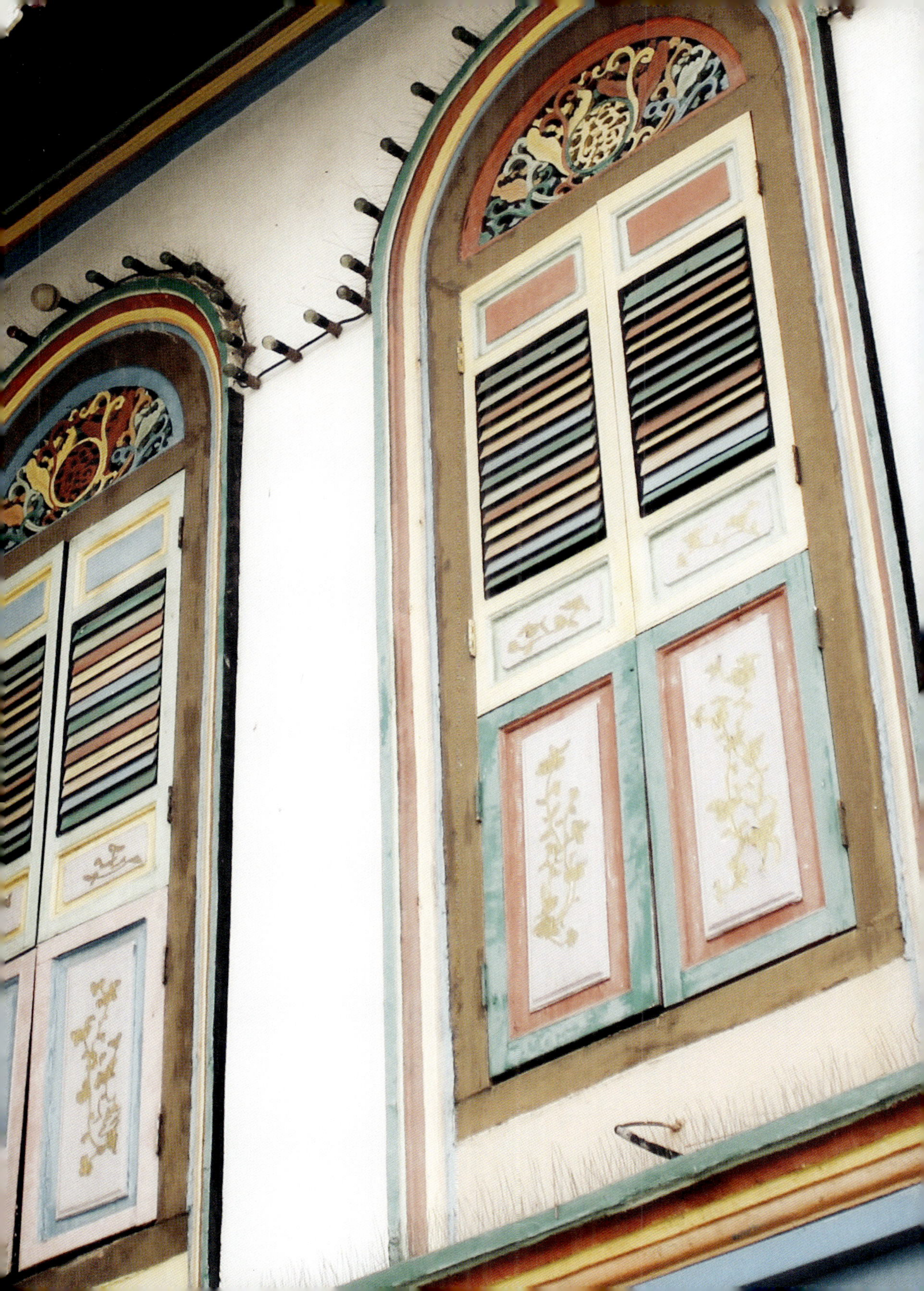

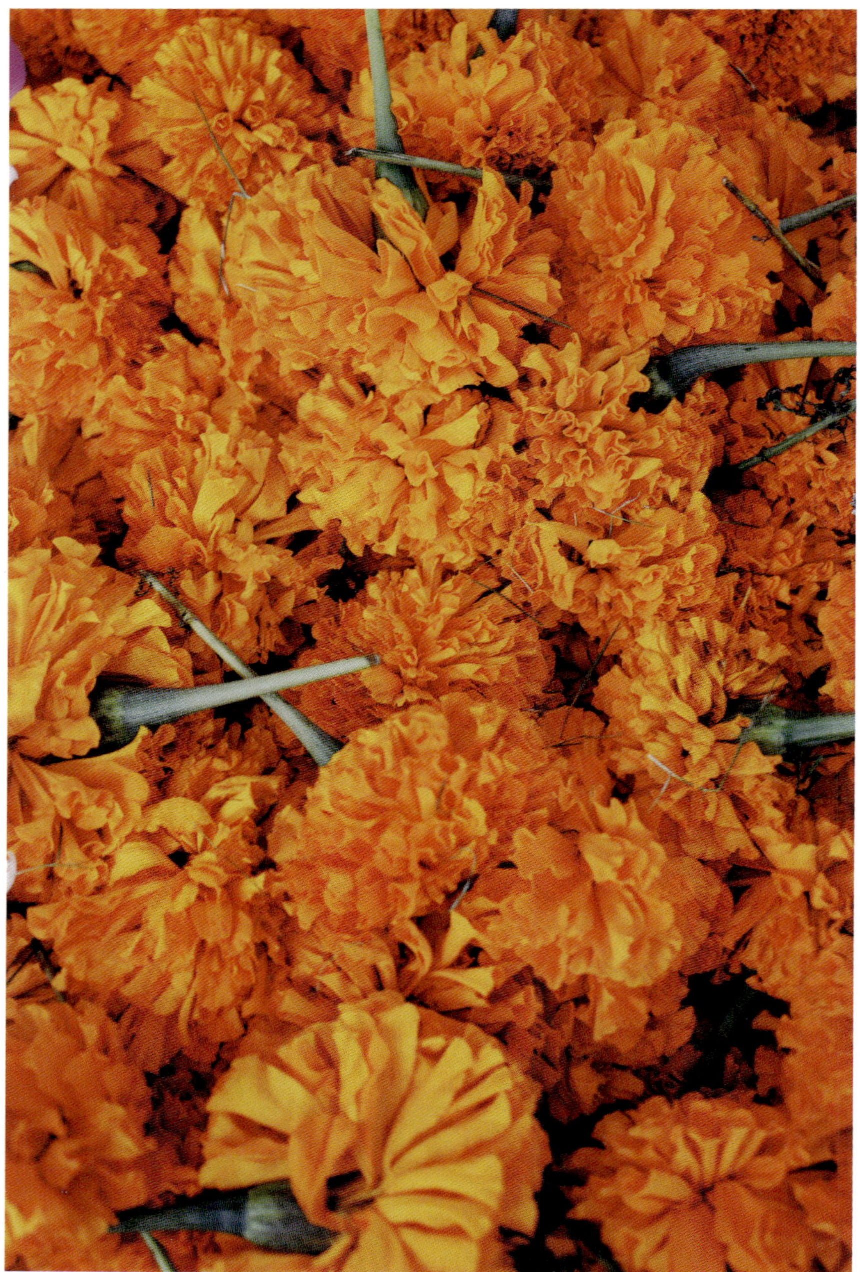

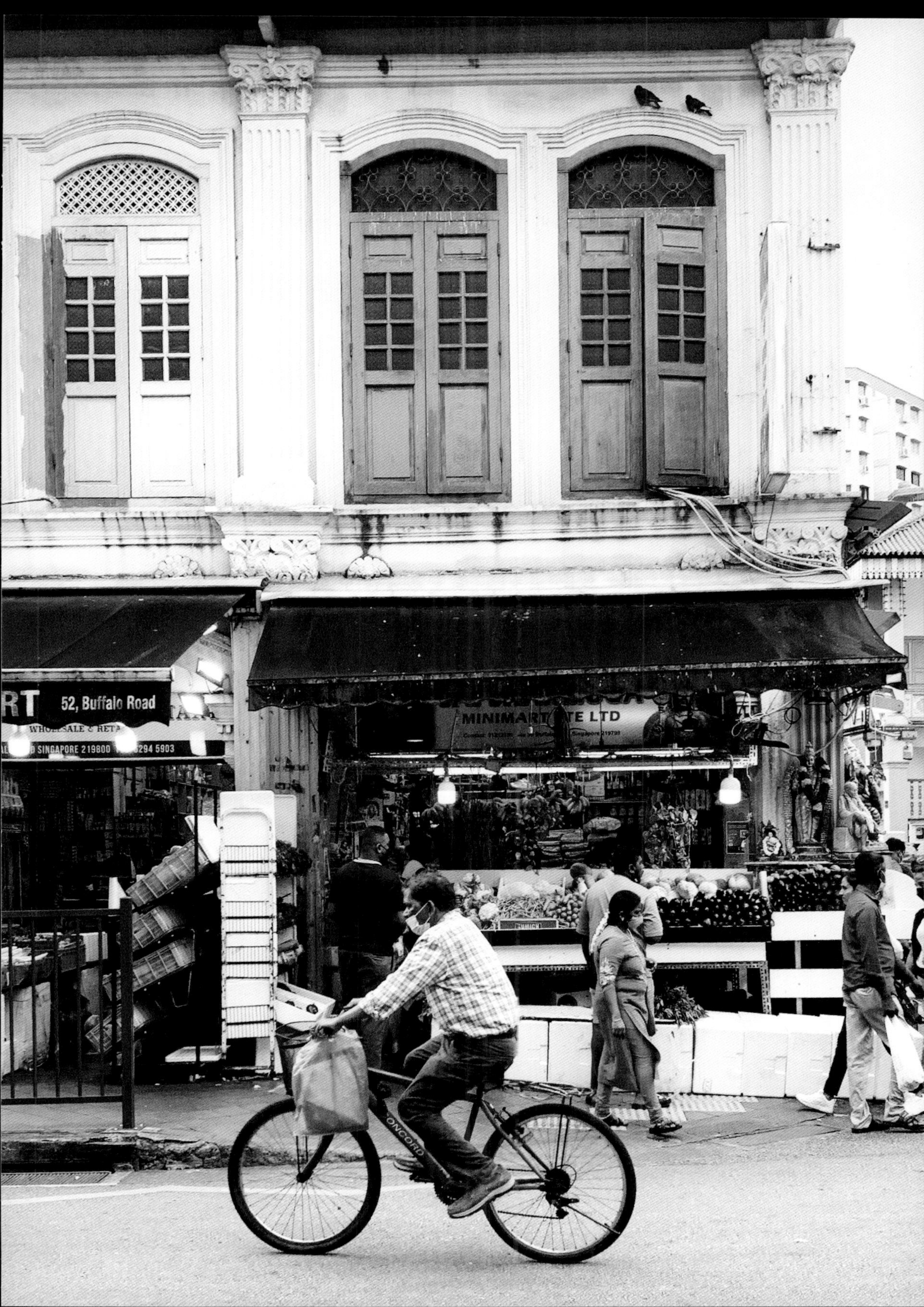
RT  52, Buffalo Road
WHOLESALE & RETA
SINGAPORE 219800    6294 5903
MINIMART  TE LTD

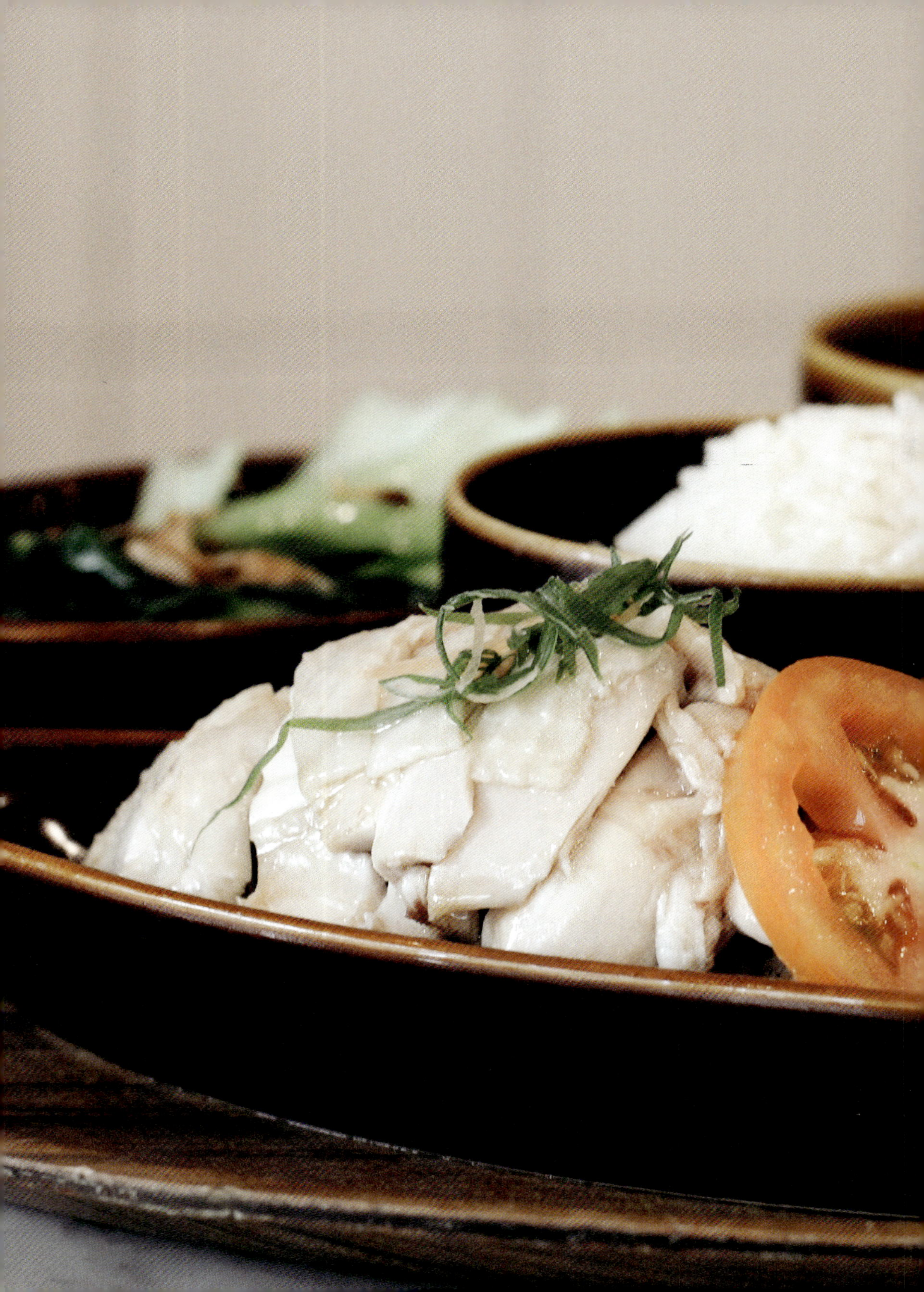

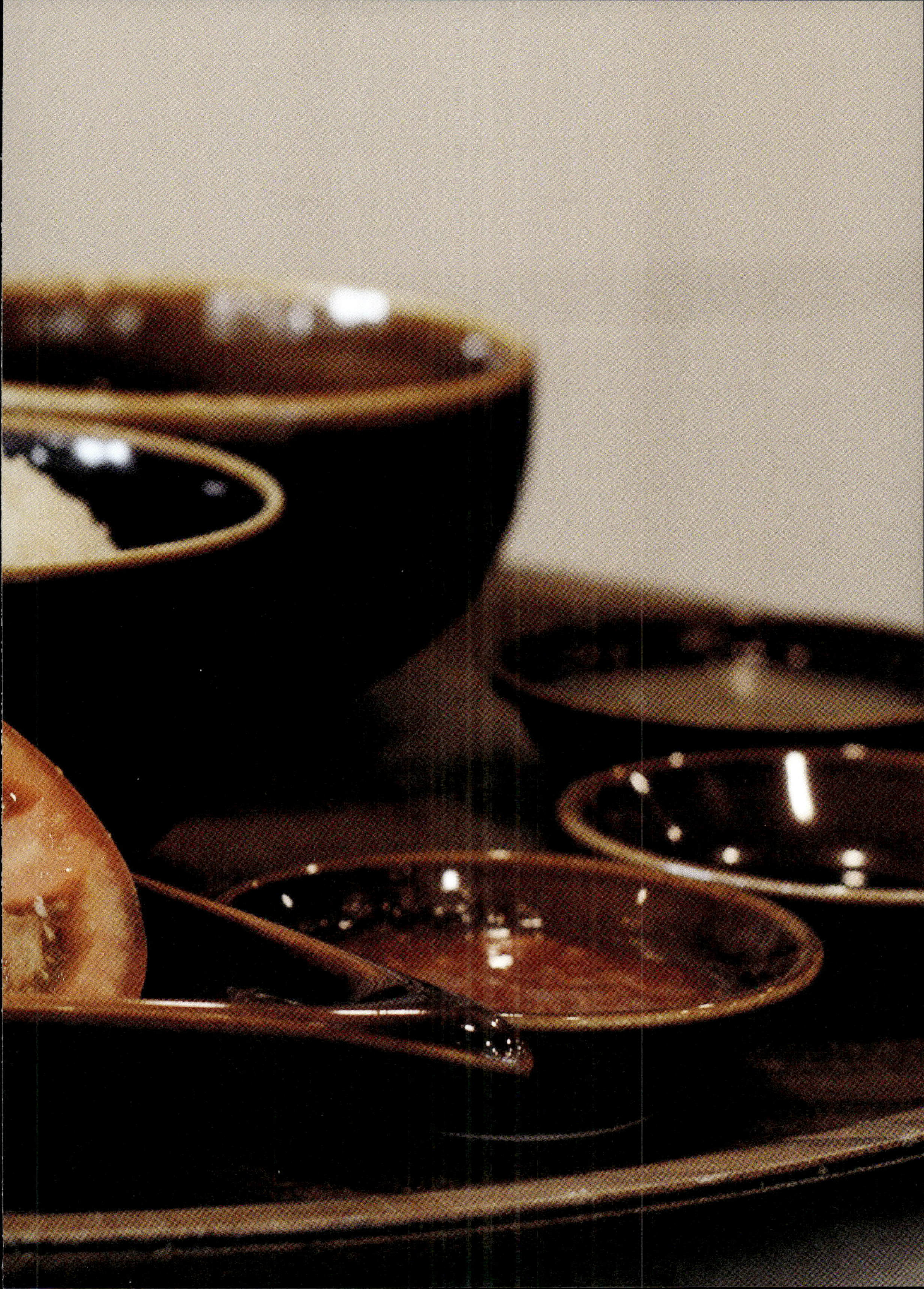

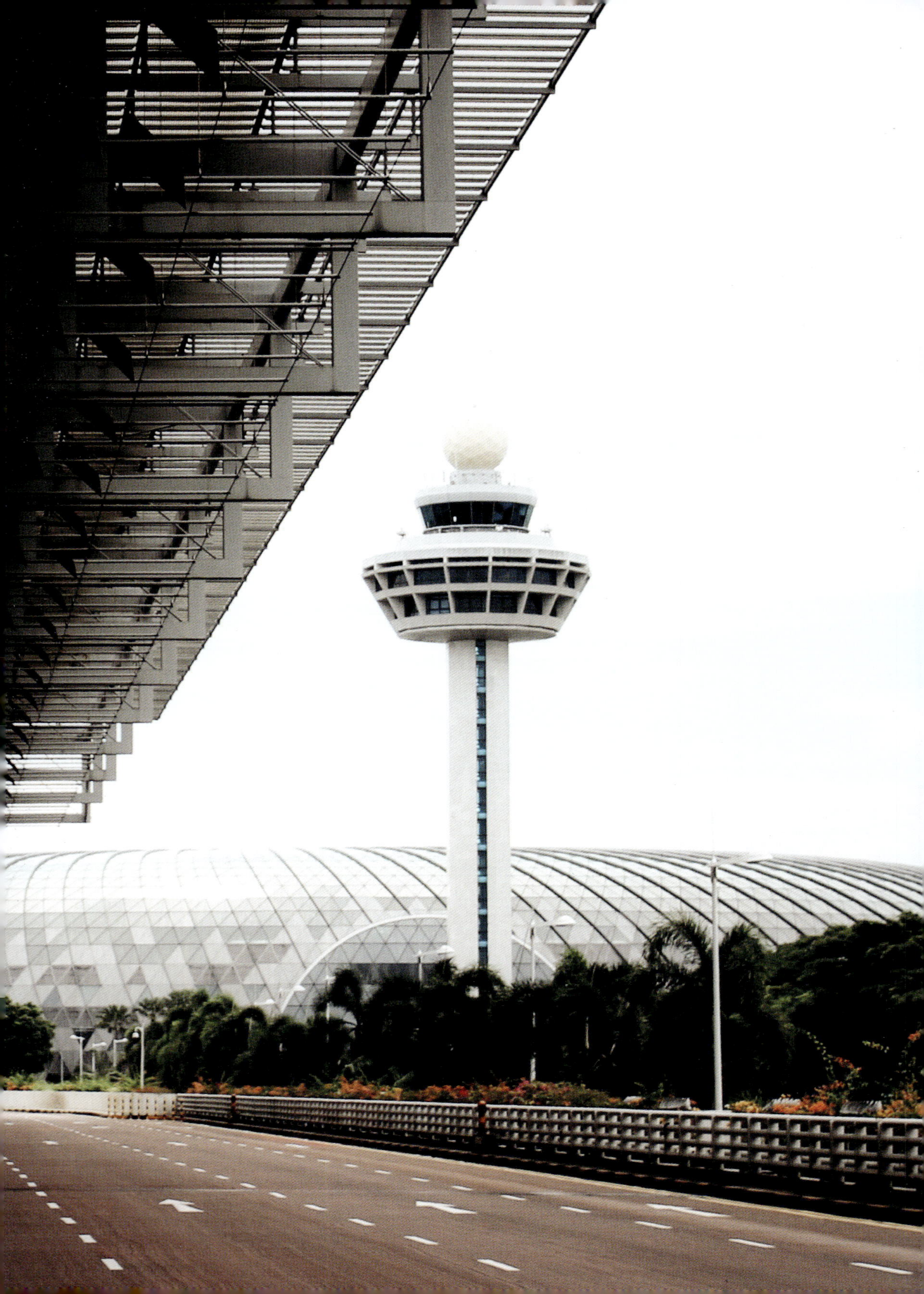

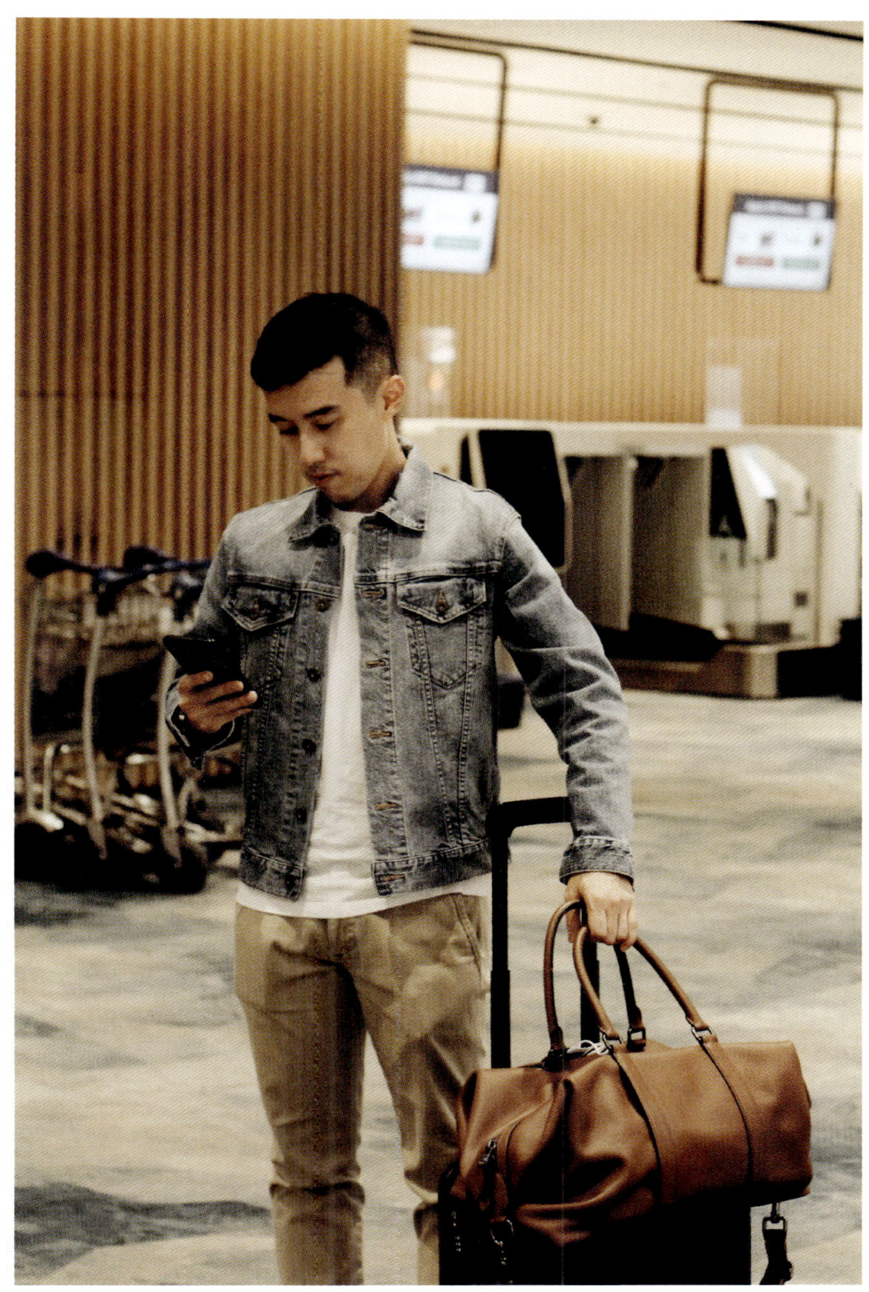



Departure

The Weekender

# SINGAPORE

Published by New Heroes & Pioneers
Photography and text: Matthew Chen
Creative Direction: Francois Le Bled
Book Design: Daniel Zachrisson
Copy Editing: Matt Porter
Model: Stefan Gerard Tan

Print and bound by BALTO print (Lithuania)
Legal deposit September 2022
ISBN 978-91-986566-0-2


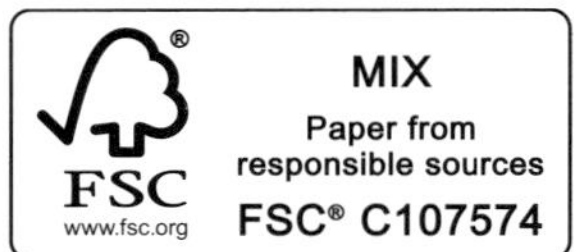





With thanks to:
Francois Le Bled, Daniel Zachrisson, Stefan Gerard Tan

The Warehouse Hotel – thewarehousehotel.com
Gibson Bar – gibsonbar.sg
Trapeze Recreation Club – trapezerec.club
Punch – punch.sg
Supermama – supermamastore.com
Hounds of the Baskervilles – hounds.sg

Lumo Restaurant and Bar – lumo.sg
The Coconut Club – thecoconutclub.sg
The Projector – theprojector.sg
SOJAO Shop – sojao.shop
Super Farmers – super-farmers.com


**COLLECTIVE SHORTS**
*by* NHP PUBLISHING